Ladner-Drysdale
Washington D.C. | London | Singapore

ISBN 0-9760662-1-1

Printed in the United States of America

Making the Connection

A PARENT'S GUIDE TO MEDICATION IN AD/HD

by Mohab Hanna, MD

LADNER-DRYSDALE

Contents

Acknowledgements

The content and format of the information presented in this guide is a result of several important factors. This guide is an outworking of the excellent training I received at the Johns Hopkins University School of Medicine. The faculty leadership of the Child and Adolescent Psychiatry Division was instrumental in providing a superior training experience. That training supplied a coherent and systematic approach to the many intricate and complex circumstances many families encounter with their children and teenagers. My gratitude is extended to the entire faculty of the Division of Child & Adolescent Psychiatry for their willingness to impart their knowledge and experience in the treatment of children and adolescents. The insight and clinical acumen of Dr. John Walkup, Dr. Mark Riddle, and Dr. Emily Frosch has been of great influence to the practice of many Child & Adolescent Psychiatrists.

I am also grateful to the many parents who have entrusted me with providing treatment to their children. This is a responsibility that I value immensely, and for which I am incredibly appreciative. The idea for this book actually sprang from the many inquiries I have received from parents looking for a useful guide about AD/HD medications. I know that many of you struggle greatly with the decisions that you must make regarding your child's treatment. I admire the thoughtfulness and research that you undertake before making significant and complex decisions.

I am thankful to the many pediatricians, therapists, and educational consultants I work with for trusting me to provide treatment to their patients. I am especially thankful to all of my colleagues at MedPsych Associates for providing a pleasant and engaging work environment. Special thanks to Dr. Barbara Kim for her expert review of the manuscript and valuable input.

There are many more people that I would like to thank, especially Marty Makary, Julie Sterling, and Sylvia Faragalla, for the different roles they played in this project. Lastly, I am most grateful to my amazing and wonderful wife, Claire, for her detailed review of the text and for her constant support as I wrote this book.

Preface

Michael is a five-year-old boy I saw several years ago for a consultation after his parents were asked to remove him from two different pre-schools. His teachers found him to be very disruptive and uncooperative. He constantly ran out of his class and frequently hit other children. The school had suggested that Michael might have attention deficit hyperactivity disorder (AD/HD) and that his parents should consider putting him on medication. The parents expressed their frustration with the situation and were very concerned about doing what was best for Michael. They had many reservations about putting their son on medication, especially since they felt they were able to handle his behavior when he was at home. They also wondered if there were other options that might help Michael, besides medication.

This scenario is played out repeatedly in many doctors' offices. The decision to put your child or teenager on an AD/HD medication is a tough one. Daily, there are reports in the media about AD/HD medications. In a recent cover article, TIME magazine posed the question: "Are we giving kids too many drugs?" The article, titled "Medicating Young Minds," highlighted the stories of several children and teenagers put on medication to help them with underlying emotional and behavioral difficulties. This article discussed several of the important, yet controversial issues, surrounding the use of medications in children and adolescents. Dr. David Fassler,

Professor of Psychiatry at the University of Vermont, noted: "We know that kids are not just little adults, they metabolize medications differently." Dr. Glen Elliott of the University of California, San Francisco pointed out: "The problem is that our usage has outstripped our knowledge base. Let's face it, we're experimenting on these kids without tracking the results." The piece went on to discuss what necessitates the use of medication, and how medication potentially benefits children and adolescents with emotional and behavioral problems.

Many articles and reports have discussed the use of medication in children and teenagers, both before and after the TIME article. The dilemma is that some reports tell us about the benefits of medication, while others talk about the dangers. In December 2004, the Food & Drug Administration (FDA) issued a warning regarding one of the commonly prescribed AD/HD medications due to concerns about potential liver problems. Two months later, Health Canada (the Canadian equivalent of the FDA) suspended all sales of another AD/HD medication amid concerns about sudden deaths of patients while on this medication. Then, in August 2005, Health Canada reversed its decision and reinstated the medication. It is becoming more difficult for parents to make medication decisions on behalf of their children. The conclusion of the TIME article was that parents must be knowledgeable and well-informed regarding their child's condition. In addition, they must be aware of the various treatment options available. This guide will enable you to make the most-informed decision regarding your child's care. Sooner or later, every parent of an AD/HD child or teenager will face a decision regarding the use of medication. This guide will prepare you with the indispensable information you need to make the right decision.

The information in this guide is presented systematically. The initial sections are the building blocks of information you will need prior to making a decision regarding treatment. Certain sections such as "Medication Rules," "Different Available Medications," and "Helpful Resources," while part of the overall context of the book, also serve as handy reference sections you'll refer to again and again.

This book is divided into five sections: Section one reviews basic information regarding AD/HD, as well as the consequences of not treating AD/HD across the life span. Section two outlines some essential rules regarding the use of medication in the treatment of AD/HD. Section three provides detailed essential information for the most commonly prescribed medications for the treatment of AD/HD. This section is divided into two parts. The first part covers the stimulant medications while the second part covers the non-stimulant medications. The sections on the stimulants and Atomoxetine are significantly larger than the other sections, primarily because more research trials have been conducted on these medications, resulting in more data. Section four covers the answers to frequently asked questions that many parents have regarding AD/HD and its treatment. The last section contains helpful resources and references for additional study. Throughout the book I have used many scenarios involving patients that I treat. The names and some of the details have been altered to protect the privacy of my patients.

Making the Connection

A PARENT'S GUIDE TO MEDICATION IN AD/HD

SECTION 1—Introduction

Part 1: Why another book on AD/HD?

Every few weeks, I receive a phone call from a concerned parent. Often, they are asking about one of the medications their son or daughter takes. The questions are usually prompted by something they heard on the news, saw in the newspaper, or read on the Internet. At other times, the question follows a conversation with a concerned friend or relative. It has become very arduous for parents to make decisions regarding their children's care. There is an inordinate amount of information that currently already exists. This book will seek to answer some of the following questions:

1) Does my child really need treatment for "this AD/HD"?
2) Should I be considering medications to help them?
3) What about all the bad stuff you hear?
4) Is it even going to make a difference?
5) How do I go about making this decision?
6) How long would they have to take this medicine?

Along with these questions, many other issues arise concerning the treatment of AD/HD. The aim of this book is to help parents make a well-informed decision regarding the treatment of AD/HD. The first significant step in making this decision is to determine whether your child or teenager even requires treatment. Once it has been decided that there is a need for treatment, an important part of making this informed decision is being aware of the available treatment options for AD/HD. Next, the strengths and weaknesses of the available treatment options must be evaluated.

The intention of this book is to empower parents with a vital understanding of the many fundamental aspects of AD/HD and its management. **This book cannot and should not replace regular visits with your child's physician.** Regular monitoring by a physician is paramount to the proper management of AD/HD, whether your child is on medication or not. It is my strong belief that parents need to take a proactive role in their child or teenager's treatment. The focal point of this book is on the potential use of medication in the treatment of AD/HD. However, regardless of whether or not medications are used, there are non-medication strategies that must also be incorporated in the proper management of AD/HD.

Every parent of an AD/HD child or teenager will face a decision regarding the use of medications.

Part 2: Understanding AD/HD

Mrs. Jones is a working mother with two children. A family friend referred her to me, out of concern for her daughter, Melissa. Melissa is a seven-year-old girl who has had a difficult time transitioning into the first grade. Melissa's teacher was concerned about Melissa's ability to focus and pay attention, and suggested to Mrs. Jones that she should have her daughter evaluated for AD/HD. Mrs. Jones is worried that her daughter will be labeled as a "bad kid" and she confessed that she is not even entirely sure what AD/HD is. Like many people, she has heard sporadic information on the radio that "too many kids have it" and some family members have told her that they think Melissa is "just lazy."

There are many people who lament that too many children are being diagnosed with attention deficit hyperactivity disorder (AD/HD). There is, in fact, a great deal of information and opinions regarding this disorder. **This is not a new condition.** AD/HD is a medical condition that has been recognized for many decades. Many names have been used in the past for this condition, including "minimal brain dysfunction." An apparent increase both in knowledge and awareness of this condition has resulted in more people being diagnosed with AD/HD.

It is becoming increasingly complicated for any parent to assess all of the information that currently exists. In order for Mrs. Jones to make a decision regarding her daughter's treatment, she first needs to fully grasp what AD/HD is and what it is not.

What is AD/HD?

Attention deficit hyperactivity disorder (AD/HD) is a complex medical condition, characterized by a cluster of three categories of symptoms: inattention, hyperactivity, and impulsivity. As would be expected, these clusters of symptoms have a negative impact on daily life. All of us will at some point have some of these symptoms, but for children and adolescents with AD/HD, these symptoms are excessive and inappropriate both for their age and for their developmental stage.

A child doesn't need to have all three categories of symptoms to have the condition. Likewise, if a child or teenager has some of the symptoms, that doesn't necessarily mean they have AD/HD. This condition has a pattern of presentation like any other medical condition; and like any other medical condition, there are differing degrees of severity. The milder the condition, the less likely it is to have a negative impact. It is also true that milder cases tend to be diagnosed later, since there are less academic and social expectations during the early school years. The reverse is also true: that the more severe the condition, the earlier the diagnosis, as the symptoms are more obvious.

How common is AD/HD?

It is estimated that between 3 and 7 percent of school-aged children have AD/HD. Many studies, however, estimate its prevalence to be even higher. It is the most commonly diagnosed behavioral disorder in childhood. Moreover, AD/HD is not a condition that only affects children. While it tends to first become obvious during childhood, for many children, this condition continues to impact their lives well into adolescence and even adulthood.

It appears to occur three to six times more often in boys than in girls. This statistic is currently being disputed. It is recognized that boys, due to hyperactivity and more disruptive symptoms, tend to get diagnosed earlier. Girls, on the other hand, who exhibit more of the inattentive, but less disruptive symptoms, tend to not get diagnosed because their inattentive symptoms go unnoticed. There are some experts who estimate that AD/HD affects both males and females equally.

What causes AD/HD?

AD/HD is a **brain-based condition** that tends to become apparent in some children in the preschool and early school years. However, there is no known precise cause of AD/HD. Like most medical disorders, AD/HD is most likely caused by a complex interaction between biological and environmental factors. However, there is a convincing body of evidence pointing to a neurobiological basis.

Studies have shown there are abnormalities in the brain anatomy, as well as in the brain chemicals of people with AD/HD.

Anatomic magnetic resonance imaging (MRI) has shown a consistent difference in the size of certain brain structures in people with AD/HD.

Genetics

There have been numerous recent studies validating a genetic component as the basis of this condition. AD/HD has been present in many families for generations. Often, parents will tell me that no one in their family has been diagnosed with AD/HD. However, when we start reviewing their family history, we discover a number of relatives who had both behavioral and academic difficulties during childhood, substance abuse and legal problems due to impulsive tendencies, a difficult work history, and relationship problems. Just because there have been no family members diagnosed with AD/HD, that doesn't mean it doesn't exist in those families.

The genetic component of AD/HD has been established in numerous studies of twins.

Environment

As stated above, most of the research points to a combination of neurobiology and genetics as the main causes of AD/HD. There are some parents who worry they somehow did something wrong, or that their parenting caused the AD/HD.

No credible evidence currently exists that AD/HD is caused purely by environmental factors, or by any specific child-rearing methods.

This does not mean that the environment has no influence on the manifestation of the disorder. Children with AD/HD in unstructured and chaotic environments do tend to have a higher degree of difficulty. Undeniably, there is a benefit to increasing structure in both the home and school environments.

No credible evidence currently exists that AD/HD is caused purely by environmental factors, or by any specific child-rearing methods.

In addition, there is a potential connection to an increased risk of AD/HD in children born to mothers who used alcohol and cigarettes during pregnancy.

Many people believe that AD/HD behaviors can be attributed to willful disobedience or to the child being "lazy" or "bad." While it is undoubtedly true that any child can, at times, be willfully oppositional or defiant, it is important to look at the AD/HD symptoms in context. For example, some kids who have AD/HD simply do not have the ability to sit down, to get their work started, and to continue to sustain their attention for certain tasks. Just like any other child, teenager, or even adult, people with AD/HD will avoid those responsibilities that are very demanding and difficult for them.

The distinction is that children and teenagers with AD/HD have less capacity and ability to compensate for those difficulties; they tend to give up more easily, and tend to avoid the required tasks altogether. This is an essential point to bear in mind.

In most circumstances, if we know what the underlying cause of any condition is, we can begin to specifically target the treatment. If we come to the conclusion that the root of the problem is "being bad" or "being lazy," then the appropriate treatment will be "punishment." If the child or teenager truly has AD/HD, this tactic will backfire. This approach will not lead to an adjustment in the negative behavior.

Punishing a child or teenager for AD/HD symptoms will result in more frustration, and not in a significant improvement of symptoms.

What about food additives and sugar?

There is no current research that shows food additives or sugar have a significant negative long-term effect on behavior or learning in children. This doesn't mean that excessive consumption of certain substances won't make some people temporarily more hyper or fidgety. As in most situations, common sense must be used here. Clearly, the excessive consumption of certain foods is not beneficial to anyone, whether they have AD/HD or not.

What are the symptoms of AD/HD?

One of the hallmarks of AD/HD is that the symptoms are always present. They are not present only at school, or only at home. They are apparent to some degree every day and all day. They don't manifest themselves during a specific season or time of year. Naturally, the symptoms tend to be more obvious in certain settings. However, AD/HD affects all aspects of someone's life. It is not just a school disorder.

There is no single objective test that is used to determine if someone has AD/HD. There are no laboratory tests such as blood or urine screens that will diagnose AD/HD.

Instead, a comprehensive diagnostic clinical evaluation must be made, as detailed later in RULE #1, Section 2 of this book. A key focus in making an AD/HD diagnosis is to evaluate for the presence of the diagnostic criteria outlined in the Diagnostic and Statistical Manual of Mental Disorders, 4th edition (DSM-IV-TR, 2000).

It is imperative to recognize that having an occasional symptom doesn't mean someone has AD/HD. Several of the symptoms associated with AD/HD are often seen in children without the disorder. The distinction is that, in children or teenagers with AD/HD, there is a significant increase in the number of symptoms. Moreover, the symptoms tend to occur more frequently, more intensely, and in more than one setting. These symptoms must significantly interfere with their function or cause problems in at least two settings such as home, school, or social situations.

There is no single objective test that is used to determine if someone has AD/HD. There are no laboratory tests such as blood or urine screens that will diagnose AD/HD.

In addition, the symptoms must be present for longer than six months. In other words, if a child displayed AD/HD symptoms for only a three-week period, it wouldn't necessarily mean they have AD/HD. There are countless plausible explanations why a person could experience difficulties in their ability to concentrate or focus for a limited period of time. A common example is that of a young child who is anxious about starting school.

According to the DSM-IV-TR, the symptoms must start before the age of 7. This does not mean that a person needs to be diagnosed with AD/HD before the age of 7. In addition, some experts assert that the inattentive type of AD/HD can present up to the age of ten or eleven.

There are plenty of people who get diagnosed as adults. In these cases, the symptoms were there while they were children, but were not recognized at the time. There are countless children with AD/HD who remain undiagnosed until their symptoms begin to interfere with their function at enough of a significant level to finally get attention. The most common scenario is that of academic difficulties; this tends to lead to the diagnostic evaluation.

AD/HD symptoms are divided into three main categories:

Symptoms of Hyperactivity:

1) Fidgets with hands or feet or squirms in seat
2) Leaves seat in classroom or in other situations in which remaining seated is expected
3) Runs or climbs excessively when inappropriate
4) Has difficulty playing or engaging in leisure activities quietly
5) Is always on the go or acts as if "driven by a motor"
6) Often talks excessively
7) In adolescents, may be exhibited by feelings of restlessness

Symptoms of Impulsivity:

1) Blurts out answers before questions have been completed
2) Has difficulty awaiting turn
3) Interrupts or intrudes on others

Symptoms of Inattention:

1) Fails to pay close attention to details or makes careless mistakes
2) Has difficulty maintaining attention in tasks or play activities
3) Does not seem to listen when spoken to directly
4) Does not follow directions and fails to complete schoolwork, chores, or, in adolescents, on-the-job duties
5) Has difficulty organizing tasks or activities
6) Avoids or dislikes tasks that required sustained mental effort, such as schoolwork or homework
7) Loses things necessary for tasks or activities
8) Is easily distracted
9) Is often forgetful in daily activities.

There are three different types of AD/HD Diagnoses:

1) Predominantly Inattentive Type: There is the presence of six or more symptoms of inattention
2) Predominantly Hyperactive-Impulsive Type: There is the presence of six or more symptoms of hyperactivity/impulsivity
3) Combined Type: There is the presence of six or more symptoms both of inattention and hyperactivity/impulsivity

Some common conditions that tend to be seen alongside of AD/HD:

1) Learning Disorders
    a. Children with AD/HD are at high risk for a learning disorder in reading, mathematics, and writing.
    b. If a learning disorder is present, there is a need for remedial education.
2) Anxiety Disorders
    a. Separation anxiety disorder
    b. Social anxiety disorder

    c. Generalized anxiety disorder
    d. Phobias
3) Depressive Disorders
    a. Can be secondary due to persistent demoralization from the difficulties associated with AD/HD
4) Behavioral Disorders
    a. Oppositional Defiant Disorder (ODD)
        i. Hostile negativistic and defiant behaviors
    b. Conduct Disorder
        i. Outgrowth of ODD
        ii. Severe negative behaviors including aggression and violence

It is crucial that your child receives a comprehensive evaluation before treatment is initiated. Just because you know the symptoms of AD/HD, does not mean that your child has it. Not every child that fidgets has AD/HD. Remember that AD/HD symptoms tend to be present in many different settings. There are many times when being fidgety is within normal childhood behavior. At times, anxious children appear to have AD/HD. In addition, not every child who has difficulty focusing has AD/HD. It could be many different things such as normal behavior, anxiety, depression, learning disabilities, etc. The key principle here is to get an evaluation before you start treatment.

There needs to be a clear understanding of the condition that is being treated.

There needs to be a clear understanding of the condition that is being treated.

Part 3: What happens if we don't treat?

In the process of making a decision regarding the use of medications, it is imperative to remember the consequences of untreated AD/HD in childhood, adolescence, and even into adulthood. This chapter will discuss some of the common consequences of not treating AD/HD that are seen during childhood, adolescence, and adulthood.

School-age children: Jessica

Jessica is an active 9-year-old girl who attends a local public elementary school. Her parents brought her in for a consultation because she was becoming belligerent every day after school when it was time to do homework. Her parents were having power struggles with her on a daily basis. She was easily distracted by everything in her room, and couldn't seem to sit down to do any of her work. Her parents were also frustrated because it seemed she never remembered to bring the right books home, and at times didn't even know what the homework was. They tried using an agenda book, but Jessica became increasingly disinterested in writing down her assignments. Her teacher was also becoming concerned that Jessica was starting to fall behind her peers in several subjects. Her parents had been alarmed about Jessica for several years, but thought when she matured, things would get better.

Comments: Jessica's story highlights some of the difficulties that school-aged children with AD/HD have. The AD/HD symptoms (distractibility, forgetfulness, difficulty with sustained attention) are beginning to get in the way of her ability to learn as well as her behavior. When schoolwork becomes difficult for some children, they may become avoidant. Their avoidance tends to be exhibited as oppositional behaviors. Listed below are some of the potential negative consequences of not treating AD/HD in school-aged children.

- School failure
  - Very little learning is taking place since the child can't focus or concentrate
  - Frequent missing assignments due to forgetfulness
- Peer rejection
  - Children with AD/HD have difficulty getting along with other children
  - This can be a result of their impulsivity, as well as their inability to learn appropriate social cues.
  - Other children and their parents avoid spending time with kids who have AD/HD because they tend to get into frequent trouble
- Social isolation
  - As a result of peer rejection and a lack of available playmates
- Demoralization, which can lead to depression
  - Children want to do well in school, but when they begin to do poorly, they tend to have an increasingly negative view of themselves and of their abilities
  - Children with AD/HD seem to always be in trouble, both at home, and at school
- Negative relationships with siblings
  - Aggression towards both younger and older siblings
  - Possibly due to the tendency of children with untreated AD/HD to become angry very quickly, and very intensely

- Oppositional behaviors
  - Frequent hostile, defiant behaviors towards authority figures resulting in numerous arguments
  - Recurrent temper tantrums or a quick and regular loss of self-control
  - Can be due to untreated impulsivity
  - Progressive pattern of learned negative interactions
- Accidents & injuries
  - Mostly due to physical impulsivity and impulsive decisions
- Hostile relationship with parents
  - Frequent power struggles
  - Increasing irritation of the parents regarding their child's difficulties
  - Frequent oppositional behaviors

Adolescents: Todd

Todd is an outgoing fifteen-year-old teenager who attends a local private high school. His parents brought him in for an evaluation because they were alarmed about his apparent lack of concern for their authority. Over the last three years, there had been a steady decline in his grades, as well as in his behavior. His parents also expressed unease about some of the friends he had been spending time with.

When Todd was in the second grade, he was diagnosed with AD/HD and placed on Ritalin® for a brief period of time, with some benefit. However, he didn't want to take it at the time, and had not received any treatment since. Although Todd was at least of above average intelligence, and had no learning disabilities, he had been barely passing most of his classes. His motivation for doing schoolwork had steadily declined over the last year; and he acknowledged that he didn't care about his grades. There had also been several incidents over the last three years. He was caught shop-lifting two years ago and put on probation. In the last few months, he had been using marijuana and alcohol on a regular basis.

When I inquired about his grades, he agreed that studying was problematic for him because he was too distracted and couldn't focus. He added that he couldn't keep up with his schoolwork because he was too disorganized and could never keep track of his assignments or even when he had tests. When he studied for exams, he tended to do well, but his grades were poor because of missing assignments. When I asked him about the shoplifting incident, he responded: "It was wrong, I was stupid, I just wasn't thinking." It was clear that by the time I saw Todd, he had become totally demoralized regarding his academic abilities, and his desire to attend college had decreased.

Comments: Todd's story highlights some of the predicaments that teenagers with AD/HD can find themselves in. Similar to Jessica in the prior story, Todd is having major problems in school. The AD/HD symptoms (disorganization, difficulty focusing, distractibility, forgetfulness) are making it very hard for him to keep up with his schoolwork. At this point, he is totally demoralized and has started making poor peer choices. His impulsivity in decision-making has already resulted in a shoplifting incident, as well as his recent use of alcohol and drugs. Listed below are some of the potential detrimental consequences of untreated AD/HD in adolescents:

- Academic failure
  - Due to lack of motivation or inability to do school work at an adequate level
  - Falling behind with school work
  - Poor performance on both regular and standardized tests
- Peer rejection
  - Many teenagers reject other teenagers on the basis of academic performance
  - Being too hyper, impulsive, and silly is perceived as immature
- Social isolation
  - Lack of available peers who are interested in friendship

- Alcohol and drug use
    - Impulsivity in decision-making
    - Peer rejection can lead certain teenagers to gravitate towards "the wrong crowd"
- Pregnancy
    - Impulsivity in decision-making
- Car accidents
    - Due to distractibility while driving, as well as making impulsive choices
    - Increased risk for speeding and unsafe driving
- Hostile relationship with parents
    - Steady pattern of negative interactions
    - Disrespect of parental authority
- Demoralization that can lead to depression
    - Academic failure
    - Peer rejection that leads to social isolation
    - Hostile relationship with parents
- Conduct disorder
    - Infringement of the basic rights of others
    - Serious breach of rules such as truancy
    - Episodes of theft such as shoplifting
    - Physical aggression towards others
    - Destruction of property

Adults: Larry

Larry is a forty-three-year-old real estate agent who lives alone. He has three children from two different marriages. He has mostly worked in sales on and off since graduating from high school. He briefly attended a local community college, but never received a degree. He has worked in many different industries, ranging from insurance to auto parts. Larry has always been well-liked by his co-workers, but has often been perceived to be irresponsible and careless. His current boss sees great potential, but is starting to get perturbed with Larry's lack of follow-through with clients. Both of his marriages ended due to financial difficulties and his checkered job history. There have been three episodes of depression: two were after each divorce, and the last one followed a recent job loss. In his early- to mid-twenties, Larry had difficulties with excessive alcohol use, and briefly lost his drivers license due to a DWI charge.

Everyone has always considered Larry to be very smart and charismatic. He did well in school until 5th grade, when he started "becoming careless and not doing his work." His parents and teachers would get very irritated because "he was so smart." Throughout high school, he was accused of being lazy and labeled a troublemaker. Despite these difficulties, he graduated from high school because "he did well when he tried."

Comments: Larry's story highlights some of the struggles that adults with untreated AD/HD have. Larry is the adult version of both Jessica and Todd. He has comparable characteristics that have affected his relationships and employments. He is intelligent, but an underachiever. His employment difficulties affected his two marriages. There have also been both legal and alcohol complications, as well as a number of episodes of depression, secondary to the detrimental life events. Adults with AD/HD tend to have trouble in their jobs due to their tendency to be disorganized and easily sidetracked, to exhibit poor impulse control in judgment, to have poor planning skills, to procrastinate, and to pay inadequate attention to details.

- Underemployment
  - Due to academic underachievement
  - In the work place, adults with untreated AD/HD come across as unreliable or unproductive
- Impaired family relationships
  - Family members find it very difficult to live with an adult with untreated AD/HD
  - Unpredictability in decisions and behaviors have a harmful impact on both marriage and parenting relationships

- Underachievement
    - Many adults with AD/HD are chronic underachievers, especially in the area of education and employment
- Legal problems
    - Often related to driving or to alcohol and drug abuse
    - Due to the inability to accurately assess the consequences of one's actions until it is too late
- Poor financial choices
    - Brought about by hasty, impulsive decisions
    - As a result of disorganization, poor planning and the inability to manage details
- Substance abuse
    - Due to diminished impulse control in judgment
    - Often secondary to all of the harmful life incidents
- Mood disorders
    - Countless detrimental life events involving relationships, employment, financial, and social expectations

The negative consequences of untreated AD/HD must be taken into consideration when a decision regarding the use of medications is being made. Of course, not everyone with AD/HD has the same level of impairment. There is a broad range of difficulties and impairments that are experienced by persons with AD/HD.

SECTION 2—Twenty-One Medication Rules Every Parent Needs To Know

This section highlights some basic principles that should be taken into account when medications are being considered as a treatment option for AD/HD. These concepts are not medication-specific, and can therefore be applied to any medication being considered. This section is designed to help you make an informed decision about AD/HD treatment. Making an informed decision about treatment is a step by step process, and these rules will help guide you through this course of action. Parents must be active participants in the decision-making process.

RULE #1

Before talking to your child or teenager's physician about starting medications, you need to know what the diagnosis is, and how the diagnosis was determined.

Richard is a thirty-five-year-old man who went to his primary care doctor, complaining of headaches. Imagine if his physician hurriedly wrote a prescription for a painkiller without asking Richard any questions, or without doing a physical exam.

Although this little scenario about Richard is an exaggeration, similar situations do occur frequently. The physician should have started by asking Richard some questions:

1) Where is the pain?
2) How long have you had it?
3) Does anything make it better?
4) Does anything make it worse?

Asking such questions would be the first step in trying to figure out what is causing the headaches. The physician would naturally examine Richard and look for any physical signs that might point to a specific cause. Certain tests might need to be ordered to help clarify the situation.

This orderly method is called the diagnostic process. It is a course of action that should be undertaken by every physician before recommending any kind of treatment.

The diagnostic process must include several basic elements:

1) Direct observation of your child by the physician
    - Your physician might observe certain behaviors in your child that would aid in the diagnostic process.
    - He also might be alerted to other issues that are present, such as tics, depression, or anxiety.
    - A physical examination should be conducted.
2) Obtaining a detailed description of the difficulties, both from you and from your child, if she is old enough to articulate the problem. Even young children can express, in different ways, what the problems are.
3) Probing for potential sources of the problem. This should include questions about:
    - Communication abilities, such as speech and language

- The presence of any unusual movements, whether voluntary or involuntary
- The ability to relate socially and get along with peers
- Gross and fine motor skills
- Learning difficulties
- Behavior in different settings
- Evidence of any mood problems
- Evidence of any anxiety symptoms
  - Specific phobias
  - Separation anxiety
  - Panic attacks
  - Obsessions
  - Compulsions
  - Avoidance behaviors
  - Performance anxiety
  - Social anxiety
- Presence of any psychotic symptoms, such as hallucinations or paranoia

4) Medical history that includes current and past medications

5) Psychiatric history

6) A family history for both the immediate and extended family that includes:
   - Medical problems that run in the family (heart disease, thyroid disease, seizures, etc.)
   - Mental health problems that run in the family (anxiety, depression, bipolar disorder, AD/HD, obsessive compulsive disorder, etc.)
   - Legal difficulties
   - Substance abuse issues
   - Educational or learning difficulties
   - Employment history

7) Educational history

8) Social history

9) Any history of trauma or abuse

10) Obtaining additional information from other sources
    - There are various behavioral checklists that can be sent to the different adults who have interactions with your child such as:
        - Babysitters
        - Tutors
        - Teachers
        - Sunday school teachers
        - Other family members
        - Neighbors
11) A neuropsychological evaluation can also be valuable in looking for the presence of AD/HD, as well as looking for the presence of other possible causes of the problem (such as a learning disability or a speech and language problem).

This entire diagnostic process can seem long and arduous, but it is impossible for your doctor to provide the appropriate treatment without first establishing a diagnosis.

Important Points to Remember:

- The diagnosis is of paramount importance, despite the amount of time and effort it will require.
- An individual symptom is not indicative of any specific condition.
    - For example, just because your child has difficulty focusing, it does not mean that he has AD/HD. Not everyone that experiences chest pain has heart disease. Clearly, more information is needed, and the entire situation must be thoroughly evaluated.
- Familiarize yourself with the criteria for AD/HD, as discussed earlier in the book.
- As stated previously, it is of the utmost importance to evaluate your child's symptoms in more than one setting (school, home, church, sports, etc.) and from multiple observers (teachers, tutors, babysitters, neighbors, etc.).

RULE #2

Medications are not the only treatment option for AD/HD, and they work best when combined with other forms of treatment.

Scott is an 11-year-old boy who has been diagnosed with AD/HD, combined type. His AD/HD symptoms clearly interfere with his academic performance, his behavior at home and at school, and result in numerous difficulties getting along with his friends. A medication trial was begun to address some of his troubles. Within a few weeks, it was apparent to everyone that Scott was better focused, less easily distracted, and less impulsive. This resulted in an improvement in his academic performance. However, he continued to struggle with his behavior at home and still found it difficult to get along with his friends. There was an obvious need for additional interventions to address these problems.

Whenever we talk about treatment, many assume that medication is the only treatment option. You need to know that medications are used to treat only the chemical aspect of the disorder and that the chemical aspect of AD/HD is only one of several components of the disorder. When medications are used, they need to be used as part of a comprehensive treatment plan that addresses:

1) Social concerns
2) Educational difficulties
3) Negative behaviors
4) Psychological and emotional difficulties

Some specific interventions may include:

1) Academic/classroom modifications
   - Some children can remain in regular classrooms with only minor interventions. This is probably most ideal and tends to be the least disruptive option. There will be a need for a teacher who is both flexible and

willing to provide some accommodations. A basic accommodation would be to provide front row seating in order to minimize distractions.

- Some children will require special educational services
  - In some instances, this can be provided within a regular classroom. There should be a specific educational plan outlined by the school, and with your collaboration, that is designed to address the specific problems your child is facing. Sometimes there is a need to pull the student out of the classroom for extra help or to provide additional needed services.
  - Some children will require a special placement outside of the regular classroom. This would entail a small teacher-to-student ratio in a structured classroom. There should be time for the student to work one-on-one with a teacher skilled in working with students with special needs.
  - In some communities, there are special schools that are designed for children with AD/HD. These schools tend to be options of last resort, but some public schools are willing to provide partial funding if they are not able to meet the needs of an individual student.

2) Behavioral modification training at home and at school
   - This is an essential component of any treatment plan for AD/HD. Occasionally, there is a need for a specific behavioral plan at school that can address learning issues, as well as negative behaviors.
     - Home interventions can include increased structure, as well as modifications to the learning environment in order to minimize distractions.

3) Evaluation for learning disabilities
   - In most public schools, the school psychologist can conduct this evaluation. Some schools will only

conduct this evaluation if your child or teenager is failing certain subjects, and some are reluctant to perform the evaluation due to limited resources. In some instances, you may need to utilize a local school advocate who can assist you with communicating your child's needs to the school.

  - If your child's school is not willing to conduct the evaluation, another alternative would be to find a psychologist in the community who has experience in this area.

4) Tutors to help with academics and organizational skills
   - You could contact the school for a list of available tutors experienced in working with students who have AD/HD. Some communities have educational consultants who specialize in working with special needs students; they tend to have training or experience in helping AD/HD students. The acquisition of organizational skills should be a component of any treatment program, and tends to have an impact on how well students function long-term.
5) Social skills training
   - This tends to be more effective when conducted in a group setting with same-age peers. However, this training can be conducted with a counselor or therapist experienced in working with children or teenagers on social skills.
6) Occupational therapy
   - This is mostly necessary for poor handwriting and other motor-related difficulties.

This list of interventions is not exhaustive; there are other recommendations beyond the scope of this guide. Please consult the reference section for other helpful resources.

The Multimodal Treatment Study of Children with Attention Deficit Hyperactivity Disorder (MTA) is a major research study that was recently conducted by the National

Institute of Mental Health. This large landmark study in children with AD/HD showed that combination treatment of medication management and behavioral treatment provided the best results for different aspects of AD/HD treatment:

1) A decrease in oppositional symptoms
2) Improved interactions between parents and their children
3) Better academic performance
4) Enhancement of social skills
5) Decrease in anxiety
6) Children who received both medication and behavioral treatment could be treated with lower doses of medicines, compared to those children who received medication treatment only, without behavioral intervention.

It is important to remember that this research study did show that stimulant medications alone had the greatest positive effect on the core AD/HD symptoms in comparison to behavioral treatments alone. However, in most instances, it is vital to address the other aspects of AD/HD that negatively impact function in different settings.

RULE #3

Medication treatment should be considered only if the AD/HD symptoms are currently impairing the child's function.

Jesse is a bright ten-year-old boy whose parents brought him to my office for a consultation because they were concerned about his lack of attention and high anxiety level. A therapist had been working with Jesse for the last nine months due to his significant anxiety, but there were also apparent AD/HD symptoms. Jesse's anxiety was negatively affecting his socialization, as well as his ability to go to school. There were many times when Jesse didn't want to go to school because of his anxiety. A decision was made to initiate a medication trial to treat the anxiety. Jesse had a very good response to the medication, and experienced no adverse effects. However, Jesse continued to exhibit clear symptoms of AD/HD, combined type.

Although Jesse was distracted in class and had trouble focusing, he was still getting very good grades. Once his anxiety was treated, he began to have more successful peer relations and no longer resisted going to school. Although Jesse was oppositional with his parents at times, they were able to set firm and consistent limits to which Jesse responded. He began using a daily written planner to help him remember his school assignments. It was decided that Jesse's AD/HD did not warrant the use of medications.

This scenario illustrates an important point. While Jesse does have both an anxiety disorder and AD/HD, medications were given only for the anxiety. The rationale behind this decision is that the anxiety problem was impairing Jesse's functioning, but the AD/HD was not. The decision to not treat the AD/HD symptoms with medication will be constantly re-evaluated as there is a possibility that at some point Jesse's AD/HD symptoms may begin to have a negative impact on his function.

When should you consider medications?

To answer that question, we must first discuss the role of medications in the treatment of AD/HD. Medications have been used to treat the symptoms of AD/HD for several decades.

Medications have the potential to improve several variables:

- Reduced hyperactivity and impulsivity
- Increased attention and concentration
- Increased accuracy of school work
- Improved social interactions
- Decreased physical and verbal aggression
- Increased compliance with adult requests
- Improved motor coordination, potentially resulting in improved handwriting

Before you consider giving your child medication, you need to evaluate the necessity of such treatment, since **the presence of a diagnosis does not automatically indicate a need for medication treatment.** Medication treatment becomes necessary if the disorder is clearly affecting a child's function. As stated earlier, children function in different spheres (school, home, peers, etc.) and all of them must be thoroughly evaluated. The story about Jesse illustrated this point. He did exhibit symptoms that were consistent with AD/HD, combined type, but these symptoms were not impacting his function enough to warrant a medication trial. For some children or teenagers, there can be a change in the degree of negative impact from the AD/HD symptoms. This can occur if there is a change in educational environment, or just because academic expectations have increased.

Don't feel pressured to use medication right away without trying to explore other potential modalities of treatment such as school intervention, organization training, social skills training, and other options.

RULE #4

The potential benefits of the medication need to outweigh the potential risks of adverse effects.

Samantha is a nine-year-old girl with a known diagnosis of AD/HD, inattentive type. Samantha's difficulties in school are secondary to her inability to focus or pay attention in class. She is very easily distracted in the classroom and while working on homework. She frequently forgets to bring her books home and, at times, forgets to hand in homework assignments. Both her teachers and her parents have become increasingly frustrated because "Samantha can do the work when she focuses." Samantha has been working with an organizational coach over the last few months, which has led to mild improvement. In addition, her parents and teachers have implemented some new strategies to help Samantha remember her school assignments. Despite these beneficial and needed changes, Samantha has continued to struggle academically.

Eventually, a decision was made to initiate a medication trial. The first medicine yielded some benefit, but Samantha became very irritable and emotional. The dose was lowered, but there was no apparent benefit. Because of the adverse effects, a different medication was prescribed. On the second medicine, Samantha again became very irritable and emotional. The same thing happened on several other medications. The lower dosing that Samantha could tolerate had no clear benefit; on the higher dose where there was some benefit, Samantha exhibited negative changes.

Samantha is evidently quite sensitive to the medications. Therefore, it became clear that the medications were not worth it. A decision was made to continue with the other interventions and to re-evaluate the use of medications in three months. This is a reasonable approach when there are obvious negative effects from the medication treatment.

To medicate your child, the potential benefit has to outweigh the potential risk of adverse effects.

Once a diagnosis has been identified and medications are being considered, a discussion with the physician regarding the various medication options should follow. A key component of this process is evaluating the positives of the medicine, versus its negatives.

Every medication has the potential to cause adverse effects, which are usually nothing more than annoying side effects that eventually disappear. However, if certain side effects persist, or cause additional negative symptoms, the medication trial should be stopped.

It is crucial that you are aware of possible adverse effects associated with the different medications and that you discuss these concerns with your child's physician. Some side effects are more common than others, and some are also more concerning than others. It is important to realize that not all side effects are tolerable, and not all go away with time.

RULE #5

Keep detailed records of all medications that your child has taken.

Robert is a 15-year-old teenager with a known diagnosis of AD/HD. Over the last two years, Robert has been doing fairly well in school. He regularly receives extra assistance from his teachers, which he finds very helpful. In addition, he meets with a tutor once a week, outside of school, to help him develop good study skills and manage his workload. Everybody agrees that Robert is a very hard worker, but "is too disorganized" and is having more and more difficulty keeping up with his increasing academic load. Robert also complains that because he has a poor attention span and is easily distracted, it is difficult for him to finish his assignments on time. Although his teachers are lenient with deadlines, Robert finds himself constantly falling behind.

Robert and his parents came to my office for a consultation to discuss the possible use of medication to address the AD/HD. Robert and his parents remembered that he had previously had one trial of medications while in sixth grade. At that time, Robert was having problems similar to those he was currently experiencing. The medication that was prescribed was both helpful and well-tolerated. In seventh grade, Robert felt that he no longer needed the medication, so a decision was made to discontinue it. In discussion with Robert and his family, we decided to restart the same medication that was previously used. The medication trial was again successful.

Robert's story illustrates the value of keeping detailed records of the different medications that have been tried, as well as their negative and positive effects. Once the need for medications has been established, the next step is to evaluate the different medication options available for treating AD/HD.

There are several important points to consider in making a decision:

1) If your child has been on a medication in the past that was well-tolerated and effective, that medication is usually a good first option.
2) Keep records of all medications that your child has been on, including the name, dosage, how long it was taken (including starting and ending date), any adverse side effects, amount of benefit, and why it was stopped. This information will be very valuable to your child's physician. When your child gets older, give him or her a copy of these records also.
3) It is best for you to keep a complete record yourself. Do not assume that your child's medical record will include all the details you may need in the future. Keep in mind that sometimes physicians move out of the area or sell their practices, making your child's file difficult to obtain or transfer.

RULE #6

Give an accurate and detailed family history.

Michelle is a 13-year-old girl diagnosed with AD/HD. She has received a variety of treatments for her AD/HD, with some success. Despite these interventions, she has been having some recent difficulties. After several discussions with Michelle and her parents, it was agreed to initiate a medication trial. The next step was evaluating the different medication options. Michelle's older sister, Amy, has also been diagnosed with AD/HD. She is currently receiving a stimulant medication that has been well-tolerated and very helpful. Upon further questioning, it was discovered that three of Michelle's cousins who have AD/HD have all benefited from the same medicine, without any major adverse side effects.

In this case, four members of Michelle's family had a good response to the same medicine with no major adverse effects. That information was helpful when it came time to decide which medication to try first. There was no guarantee that Michelle would tolerate the same medicine, or benefit from it. However, the fact that four of her family members had a positive response to this particular drug increased the likelihood that Michelle would have a similar positive experience.

Erick is a nine-year-old boy from a family with five children. Erick was recently diagnosed with AD/HD after a thorough evaluation. Erick's father, older sister, aunt, and cousin have all been diagnosed with AD/HD as well. All four of them have been tried on several medications. Moreover, all have experienced "increased nervousness and agitation" on the same medication.

Again, this type of information regarding family history is valuable in determining which medication to start with. Here we have a scenario where a particular medication caused a specific adverse effect in the rest of the family members. It would clearly be more prudent to start Erick's medication trial with a different medication. This does not mean that Erick won't have a similar type of reaction to another medicine, but it would still be wise to try a different medication first.

If a family member has been, or is on a medication that has worked well, and that medication was also well-tolerated, there is genetic evidence that this same medication would be a reasonable option for the child.

There is also a need to give an accurate family history of any medical or psychiatric problems such as tics, anxiety, or

mood disorders. This type of information is only a helpful guide in making a decision. At times, members of the same family do have different responses to certain medications, but it is more likely that members of the same family will have a similar type of response.

It is imperative that you relay to the physician as accurate a family history as you can gather. For example, if Adderall unmasked tics in your nephew, it would be worthwhile to report that information to your physician.

RULE #7

Some medications have the potential to worsen underlying problems.

Kyle is an eight-year-old adopted boy who lives with both of his parents. Over the last four years, it has become gradually apparent that Kyle has AD/HD, combined type. There have been increasing difficulties, both at home and at school. His mother has expressed concern that Kyle has very few friends. In the last few months, Kyle has been having crying tantrums before going to school. Last week, there were two days when he became very agitated and refused to go to school. Kyle indicated that he was very stressed at school and that he hated going "because it is too hard and nobody there likes me."

Prior educational testing had revealed that Kyle's intelligence was in the above-average range with no specific learning disabilities. Additional test results were consistent with the diagnosis of AD/HD. Kyle's father stated, "Kyle gets stressed easily and sometimes worries too much." Furthermore, he would often avoid doing things that he thought would be too difficult.

Kyle displays symptoms of anxiety in addition to the AD/HD. The presence of the underlying anxiety is an important consideration in deciding on a possible medication trial.

Some of the medications that are used to treat AD/HD can have the potential negative effect of increasing underlying anxiety. This can also happen if there is an underlying mood or tic disorder. In these situations, a thorough analysis of the potential benefit of medication treatment, versus the potential adverse effects, is in order.

Another variable in choosing a medication is the presence of any other concerns that are present in addition to the diagnosis of the AD/HD. **Some medications could possibly lead to the emergence of negative symptoms or behaviors that are below the surface.** A good example of this is the propensity of stimulant medications to exacerbate underlying anxiety or obsessive-compulsive behaviors. In such situations, the negative effects of a medication outweigh its overall benefit.

RULE #8

Not everything that happens while your child is on medicine is because of the medicine.

Johnny is a 12-year-old boy who has AD/HD. Three weeks ago, he was started on a medication trial. One week after starting the medication, he developed a sore throat and a fever that resolved in three days without any treatment. The cause was a virus, but Johnny's parents were concerned that the medication had contributed to the fever and the sore throat.

It turned out that there were several other children in Johnny's class who had developed a viral infection around the same time. In this case, it is highly unlikely that the medication was the cause of the symptoms.

David is an eight-year-old boy with AD/HD. He began a medication trial seven days ago. Four days after starting the medication, he did poorly on a spelling test. His parents expressed concern that the medication had contributed to his poor performance.

When I met with David, I asked him what had happened on his test. He readily admitted that he had not studied because he had a soccer game the night before that finished late. By the time he got home, he had totally forgotten about the spelling test the next day. In this case, it was certainly possible that the medicine could have caused an adverse side effect like insomnia that resulted in David being exhausted when he was taking his spelling test, but it is very important to remember that **not everything that happens while your child is on medicine is a result of the medicine.**

Maria is a 15-year-old girl with AD/HD, inattentive type. A medication trial was initiated two months ago due to her increasing difficulties in school. When she was seen recently for a follow-up appointment, she complained that she had forgotten to hand in many of her homework assignments, and that she had been easily distracted in class. She was concerned that the medication was causing her symptoms.

I reminded Maria that her symptoms stem from the AD/HD, which is the reason the medication trial was begun in the first place. The actual issue, then, was that the current medication regimen was apparently ineffective. On occasion, symptoms that are exhibited are due to the disorder that is being treated, meaning that the symptoms are being manifested despite medication intervention. The effectiveness of the medication regimen should be re-evaluated.

RULE #9

Don't expect medications to fix every symptom.

Amanda is a ten-year-old girl who was brought in with her parents for a medication consultation. The family informed me at the outset that I was the fourth physician they had seen in the last six months. Amanda had been tried on five different medications, all with very mixed results. It was obvious that both Amanda and her parents were very frustrated.

Two years ago, Amanda was diagnosed with AD/HD, inattentive type. Her school performance had always been inconsistent. Amanda had difficulty focusing, was easily distracted, forgetful and disorganized. Several of the medications that she had tried did help her to focus better, and to be less distracted. While there was some improvement in her academic performance, she still struggled with organization and still sometimes forgot to turn in assignments.

Amanda's story is not uncommon. The medications helped with some of the symptoms, but not all of them. In Amanda's case, she tolerated the medications without any adverse effects and actually did receive some benefit, but there were still other difficulties related to the AD/HD that were not being helped. Amanda's treatment history included only medication trials, without any other interventions. In cooperation with Amanda's school, we developed a treatment plan to address the disorganization and missing assignments. It was important to explain to Amanda's teachers that she was not being lazy or oppositional, but that she needed extra assistance in this area.

Medications are not magic pills; they cannot relieve every symptom.

There are times when your child will still have some symptoms, despite adequate and appropriate medications. The impact of those symptoms will vary with each child. The goals of treatment can also vary depending on your child and his or her given situation. It is always important to periodically re-evaluate the goals of medication treatment. Every child is unique and has their own special strengths and challenges. It is not reasonable to compare your child or teenager to other children with AD/HD and how he or she is performing. This can have very damaging effects on your child, and can lead to unrealistic expectations from treatment.

There are some situations in which parents have idealized or impatient expectations of treatment. This can trigger multiple medicine changes and provider changes, as well as a great deal of frustration. I have seen children end up on numerous medications, and on very high doses of medications, as a result of their parents' faulty objectives. It is important to discuss with the prescribing physician the goals of medication treatment for your child. Always keep in mind that medication treatment needs to be part of a more comprehensive treatment plan (see Rule # 2).

Children and teenagers with AD/HD are not all the same. Maintain realistic expectations of treatment based on the individualities of your child.

RULE #10

Having a side effect does not always mean it is necessary to stop the medication.

Sheila is a 17-year-old teenager who has AD/HD, combined type. Sheila received medication for the treatment of her AD/HD throughout her middle school years. She wanted to stop the medication when she started high school. Recently she asked to go back on the medication because she noticed she was having difficulty concentrating, both in the classroom and while driving. She found that she was being easily distracted. After a lengthy discussion about the possible use of medications, it was decided to start a medication trial. Within a week, Sheila noticed a difference in her ability to focus in school and while driving. The only problem was that she also began having difficulty going to sleep. We decided to do a different medication trial. Once again, there was a noticeable benefit, but the insomnia remained.

Sheila's dilemma is not that unusual. Sheila liked the fact that the medication was beneficial, but getting an adequate night's sleep was also important. We had to decide if the benefit from the medication was more important than her difficulty falling asleep. Sheila and her parents decided to continue with the medication. At times Sheila needed to use an over-the-counter sleep aid to help her sleep.

There are going to be times when there is both a clear benefit and a clear adverse effect to the medication that is being used. You need to decide if there are any adverse side effects that you are willing to live with because the benefit of the medication is so great. There are certain situations when the benefit of the medicine is so obvious that it is worth dealing with the side effect to continue taking it. There are also situations when there is a need to treat the adverse effect, such as the insomnia, brought on from the stimulants. As in most situations that arise during a medication trial, the decisions you make will be based on your child's individual needs.

At times, it is reasonable to continue to take the medication despite the presence of certain adverse side effects.

RULE #11

The medication dosage amount is important.

Daniel is a 13-year-old boy with a reported diagnosis of AD/HD. I first met Daniel two years ago when he came in with his father for a medication consultation. Both Daniel and his father were very frustrated with the ineffectiveness of the numerous different medications that had been tried.

Whenever I come across a situation like Daniel's, I know that it is imperative to perform a thorough diagnostic evaluation; it is always possible that Daniel doesn't even have AD/HD. In Daniel's case, he really did meet all the criteria for AD/HD, combined type.

After confirming the diagnosis, we needed to come up with a comprehensive treatment plan that could address Daniel's different needs. In this case, a medication trial was indicated. I reviewed with the family the different medications that Daniel had tried. There was a common theme to all of the trials: "Nothing happened!" In other words, there were neither adverse effects nor benefits. Daniel and his father both assured me that he actually did take the medications. Upon further investigation, it became clear that all of the medication trials that were tried were at a very low dose. As a matter of fact, Daniel had never been on a therapeutic dose (enough of the medicine) to see any effects, positive or negative.

Daniel's situation was a clear example of how the dosage (amount) of the medication being prescribed is very important. **A common reason why some medications are ineffective is because the dosage given is too low.** Of course, it is also true that the lowest effective dosage should be used.

A good principle is to start with a low dose and proceed slowly with increasing the dose of the medication to an effective level, but to not under-dose.

To be able to truly evaluate the effectiveness of a medication, enough of it needs to be taken for a long enough period of time. In other words, taking a medication for only one day is not going to give you enough information to be able to assess the effectiveness of the medication.

Once a medication has been started, medication trials can last from between one day and six to eight weeks. The purpose of the medication trial is to evaluate efficacy (how well the medicine works) and tolerability (anything bad happening from the medication). These are the two variables that are being examined. In order for a medication trial to be continued, there needs to be both clear efficacy (proof that it is working) and reasonable tolerability. In other words, if a medication is well-tolerated, but the efficacy is unclear, it is probably best to do a trial with a different medication. The other situation is also true; if a medication has clear benefits but is not well-tolerated, it is reasonable to do a trial with a different medication.

The main point to remember is that in order to accurately assess efficacy, the medication needs to be taken at a therapeutic dose for an adequate period of time.

RULE #12

Medications that are not specifically FDA-approved for children can still be used by children in certain situations.

I received a recent phone call from a concerned parent because her child's pediatrician had started her daughter on a new medication. The mother investigated the medication and found that it was "not recommended for use in children."

This is a situation that is important to understand. There is a great deal of misunderstanding regarding the process of medication approval, and especially when it is dealing with children and adolescents. This is an important discussion to have with your child's physician regarding the specific medication that is being prescribed. This is true for any medication, not just medications that are used in the treatment of AD/HD.

When the FDA approves a medication, it means the pharmaceutical company that makes the drug submitted research evidence that the drug is effective and safe in the group of people that were studied. This can be a very long and extensive process.

Whenever there is an age limit put on a medication, it means that the researchers did not include individuals younger than the age limit in their studies.

It does not mean that it is dangerous; it just means that the younger age group was not specifically studied. There are many medications that are used by children that are not specifically FDA-approved for children, but are used "off-label." This is a common practice in all clinical medicine. Once the FDA gives its stamp of approval, the drug company can then **market** the medication for the specific patient population in which the drug was studied; however, physicians are allowed to prescribe that medication in any situations they think are clinically appropriate. Other evidence can be used by your doctor to make a decision to treat.

Although the FDA has encouraged increased research in children, there are still many medications that are frequently used without a specific FDA approval in children ("off-label"). Physicians are allowed to prescribe most medications to children without the specific approval for children. Of course, all of these medications were approved for use in adults.

The reason these medications are used with children is that there is a great deal of information that is obtained from the actual daily practice of medicine. There are also published research studies that demonstrate the effectiveness and safety of these medications, but these studies were not related to the FDA approval process that the drug company undertook.

This issue further highlights the urgent need for more research in the child and adolescent populations. The good news is that currently the most common medications that are used in the treatment of AD/HD have in fact been FDA approved for use in children and adolescents.

RULE #13

Tell your physician all of the medications that your child is on, including over-the-counter medications and "natural" or "herbal" medications.

Jack is a 12-year-old boy with a known diagnosis of AD/HD. He has been on medication for several years with a clear benefit, and no major adverse effects. Jack has also had a long history of allergies. He was recently tried on a new medication for his allergies. His mother began noticing increased irritability and hyperactivity. Jack also became more lethargic and began having difficulties in school. His mother was concerned that the AD/HD medication was no longer effective. When the situation was examined more closely, it became clear that Jack's recent difficulties coincided with the initiation of the new allergy medication. The pediatrician was consulted and agreed to stop the allergy medication for a few days in order to monitor the situation. Within a few days, the symptoms subsided and a new allergy medication was started with no problem.

At times, your child will be on medications for other medical illnesses. It is imperative that you tell the physician all of the different medications that your child is on (for example: medications for asthma or allergies, antibiotics, etc.) including over-the-counter medications and "natural herbal" medications.

It is also important to alert your physician of any subsequent medications that have been added once the medication trial has been initiated.

RULE #14

Involve your adolescent in the discussions about medications, and be patient with them through the process.

Cindy is a 17-year-old soccer player who is well-liked by many of her peers and teachers. Cindy was diagnosed with AD/HD, inattentive type, at the age of ten. She has utilized the services of an organizational coach on and off since then. She has also had several medication trials with some benefit. When I saw her with her parents for a consultation, her junior year in high school had gotten off to a rocky start. Both Cindy and her parents were concerned about her prospects of getting into a specific college. Cindy acknowledged that she was a good soccer player, but not good enough to play on the college level. Cindy was very interested in international business, and was considering pursuing that field in college.

Her parents were interested in initiating a medication trial because "she gets good grades when she takes them." Cindy had several concerns regarding the medications and was not sure she wanted to take them again. She was primarily worried that they would change her personality. After I addressed some of her concerns, she agreed that it was worth a try.

Cindy and her parents returned for an appointment several weeks later. Her parents were frustrated at her lack of progress in school; she was still continuing to have difficulties finishing her work, both at school and at home. When I spoke to Cindy alone regarding her experience on the medication, she embarrassingly admitted that she never actually took the medication. It turned out she had more questions and concerns about them.

This resulted in a very fruitful discussion with both Cindy and her parents regarding Cindy's goals. I asked Cindy to come up with some short-term goals, as well as long-term goals. This gave us an opportunity to discuss the potential role of the medications in helping her achieve some of those goals.

One of the most common reasons why medication trials are not successful is that the medicine is never actually taken. This can be a significant concern with adolescents. It is imperative that there is open dialogue with teenagers about why they are on the medications. At times, there needs to be a great deal of patience and education with adolescents regarding the medication.

Open discussions about the teenager's short-term and long-term goals can help them understand the potential role of the medication. You should be aware that these types of discussions might result in deciding to not initiate a medication trial. However, the manner in which these discussions are handled can build the foundation for future decisions regarding medication treatment. It is also true that many teenagers do change their mind once they appreciate the consequences of not treating their AD/HD.

I realize that this approach can be difficult for many parents. However, forcing teenagers to take medication generally results in more hostility and anger about treatment and resentment towards the parents. There are some teenagers who will go to great lengths to sabotage treatment in order to prove that the medications are not helpful. The last thing you want to do is to get into a major power struggle with your teenager regarding the medication. Including them in the decision-making process is vital, but it does not mean that you shouldn't have reasonable consequences for the negative behaviors that result from not taking the medications. Again, there should be a balance of how these situations are handled, and the decisions you make should be based on your teenager's individual needs.

RULE #15

For most children, parents should be responsible for administering the medications; starting in the mid- to late-teens, most teenagers can begin to assume some of that responsibility.

Mark is a 13-year-old boy I have been treating for three years. His AD/HD symptoms responded very well to medication treatment. At a recent visit, both he and his mother indicated that things had not been going very well at school. As I began to evaluate the situation, it became clear that Mark had been missing his morning medication dose with increasing frequency. It turned out that in the last two months, Mark had assumed responsibility for his own medications. Mark admitted that he knew he needed to take the medications and he recognized their clear benefit, but by the time he realized that he had forgotten to take them, his school day was half over.

Children and adolescents with AD/HD tend to be forgetful about many different things, including taking their medicines. It is not reasonable to think that your nine-year-old child with AD/HD is going to remember to take his medicine every morning.

It should be the parent's responsibility to administer the medication to the child.

During mid- to late-adolescence, there needs to be a transition when your adolescent can begin to assume some of the medication responsibility. This needs to be done in a systematic fashion. Expect some initial difficulties in the process, but provide guidance and direction.

This could provide many opportunities for teaching your teenager certain essential skills. Some teenagers will begin to learn a variety of ways to remember doing certain important tasks such as taking their daily medication.

There are certain situations when it is not advisable for some teenagers to assume this responsibility. This clearly needs to be evaluated on an individual basis. It is advisable to discuss your specific situation with the treating physician.

RULE #16

Don't look for a quick fix; be patient.

Jane was an active nine-year-old girl that I recently evaluated for the presence of AD/HD. She had been having increasing difficulties at school, both in her academics as well as her behavior. As the evaluation process progressed, it became apparent that Jane did, in fact, have AD/HD, combined type. After several discussions with the parents regarding medication use, it was decided to initiate a medication trial with a stimulant medication. Since Jane had never been on any medications, she was started on a very low dose. Two days after the medication was started, her father called in frustration and asked if we should consider switching the medication. During our discussion, I asked if she was having any adverse effects. It turned out that Jane wasn't experiencing any adverse side effects, but "she wasn't any better."

I reassured the father that Jane was on a very low dose of the medication, and that during this initial part of treatment, we were monitoring her for any adverse effects. Once it was clear that she was tolerating the medicine, we would begin to increase the dose accordingly.

This story highlights several important points. It is imperative that you have realistic expectations regarding medication treatment. It is also essential to remember that AD/HD is a long-term condition. It is essential to be patient during the initial phases of medication treatment. There are numerous situations when the lack of patience of either the physician or the parent leads to unnecessary medication changes or unnecessarily high doses of medications. Your doctor should tell you in advance when to expect maximum benefit.

Usually, it is necessary to start the medicine at a low dose and increase it slowly. This is especially true if your child has never been on any kind of medication for AD/HD. When your child first starts a medicine, that is the time to evaluate how well they are tolerating it. The goal during the initial part of treatment is to look for any side effects.

There were two weeks left in the school year when I was asked to evaluate Marcus, a 17-year-old young man who was supposed to be graduating from high school. The problem was that Marcus was failing most of his classes. The situation seemed dire since Marcus had fallen behind in all of his classes. When I met Marcus and his parents there was an obvious urgency and apprehension regarding the situation. The parents asked if there was a "pill to help him graduate."

Marcus had struggled academically throughout high school, but he always did enough work to pass all of his classes. The result of the evaluation was consistent with a diagnosis of AD/HD, inattentive type. Both Marcus and his parents were very invested in finding the "magic pill to graduate."

Don't look for a quick fix. Your child's medications are not magic pills.

Rarely do emergency situations arise where there is an urgent need for a quick fix. There may be situations like the one Marcus is facing, where it seems there is a need for emergency intervention and you have to make a hasty decision on the spot regarding the use of medications.

In those situations, it is essential to remember that AD/HD is a long-term problem with a long-term solution. There is no "magic pill" or quick fix.

For Marcus, it made sense to begin a medication trial, but the same basic principles needed to be followed. There was no guarantee that Marcus was going to tolerate the medication, so he was started on a low dose of a stimulant. In fact, Marcus did not tolerate the initial medication that was started, and there was a need to do a trial with a different stimulant medication. Marcus ended up needing to go to summer school in order to graduate. He received intensive tutoring with an organizational coach along with the medication trial. He ended up going to a local community college for a year before he transferred to a four-year college.

As a parent, you should never feel that you have to make a decision on the spot regarding the use of medications. Refer to Rule #21 for a more detailed discussion about this immensely important point.

RULE #17

Begin new medications only when at least one parent is available to monitor any negative effects.

Several months ago, I had the opportunity to evaluate James regarding the possible use of medication intervention to treat his AD/HD. James is a nine-year-old boy who had been diagnosed with AD/HD several years before, but had been able to function well without the use of any medications. Since he recently had been having more difficulties, his parents wanted a medication consultation.

After I completed the evaluation, it was decided to initiate a medication trial with a stimulant medication. I saw James and his parents for a follow-up appointment several weeks later. When I attempted to assess how things were going on the medication, it became clear I wasn't going to get enough information. James wasn't sure if he had noticed any adverse side effects, and he generally wasn't very accurate in remembering any details. His parents were not sure how he was doing on the medication, because they had been out of town most of the time James was on the medication.

In this case, it was difficult to accurately evaluate the medication trial. As stated previously, the goal of the medication trial is to evaluate for the presence of any adverse side effects and to determine how well the medication is working.
As a parent, you are going to be the best observer of that information since you know your child or teenager better than anyone else. It is optimum that medication trials are started during a period when you can closely observe your child. If your child has never been on a certain medication, it is best to not give it for the first time if you are not going to be around.

It is always best to begin the medication on a weekend when you can monitor your child throughout the whole day.

It is imperative that there is close parental monitoring during the first several weeks of the medication trial.

When a medication is started, the main concern should be monitoring for any adverse effects, and any unexpected situations such as allergic reactions. If your adolescent drives, he or she should not drive for several days after taking the medication, until it is clear that there are no negative effects. It is also not wise to start a medication trial several weeks before your child goes away for any extended period of time, for example, to summer camp.

Every child's experience is unique when it comes to taking medications. Just because a cousin or a sibling had no adverse side effects from a medicine, does not mean it can't or won't happen to your child.

Monitoring your child or teenager closely during initial use of medications is both helpful and necessary to be able to accurately evaluate the medication. Once the medication trial has started, your goal is to gather as much information as possible to help your child's physician evaluate the medication's effect.

RULE #18

Closely note baseline sleep, appetite, and mood prior to initiating a medication trial.

Janice is a 15-year-old teenager who was diagnosed with AD/HD, inattentive type, by her pediatrician when she was seven years old. She has done reasonably well on two different medication trials. Several months ago she was restarted on one of the medications that had been both effective and well-tolerated in the past.

Her parents requested a medication consultation because they were becoming increasingly concerned about Janice's irritability and difficulty in falling asleep. The medication that Janice was restarted on did have the known potential to cause both insomnia and irritability. Both Janice and her parents confirmed that when this same medication was tried three years ago, Janice did not experience irritability or insomnia.

Several important points emerged during this discussion. It turned out that Janice had been going to bed late for the last two years. She noticed that she was getting tired later and having trouble getting up in the morning—a typical teenage sleep pattern. Her sleep pattern was exactly the same prior to initiating the medication trial. Janice also noted that even on the days that she did not take her medication, she went to bed late.

The irritability was a different matter. Even Janice's friends had noticed that she was more irritable than usual. She was always known as an easygoing girl who everybody liked. It became clear that the irritability had been present only since she started taking the medication. Janice also felt that she was not irritable on the days that she didn't take the medication.

There are some important things to note before you put your child or teenager on a medication. It is important to note their baseline eating and sleeping habits since many medications can affect both sleep and appetite. By "baseline," we mean their eating and sleeping habits before they began taking the medication. It is essential to remember that many people with AD/HD can also get irritable and experience mood changes.

Note if there is any pattern to these mood changes with respect to the time of day or if it is mostly situational. This will be very valuable if you choose to start a medication trial. Gathering some baseline information prior to initiating medications will help differentiate what is the disorder you are treating, and what is the effect of the medication. This information will also help guide your child's physician in making appropriate decisions.

RULE #19

The more times a medicine needs to be taken, the higher the risk of missing a dose.

Melanie is a 16-year-old girl I recently saw for a consultation regarding her AD/HD medications. Melanie was diagnosed with AD/HD, combined type, at the age of nine. Melanie is on a medication regimen that requires her to take the medication four times a day, including once at school. She has continued to struggle in her afternoon classes because half of the time she forgets to go to the nurse to get her medication. There are also many nights when she struggles with her homework, because by the time she remembers to take her medication, it is too late into the evening.

Melanie's story is very common for many kids and teenagers who have to take their medication several times a day (this is probably also true of most adults). In this scenario, it is possible that if Melanie forgets to go to the nurse, she could be called out of class to go to the nurse's office. Of course, most teenagers will not like the idea of being pulled out of class to "go get their medicines." As far as the after-school dose, it would be important for Melanie to have a set routine that involves taking that medication. Sometimes written reminders in prominent places are very helpful. The difficulty with some of these mid-day doses is that many teenagers with AD/HD are forgetful.

Some medications are given once a day, while others are given two to four times a day. **The more often a medication needs to be administered, the more likely a dose will be forgotten.** There is usually more adherence to treatment with medications that are taken once a day at the same time every day. If there is a need to take a medicine more than once a day, develop a routine and structure to remember to take those extra doses. For teenagers, this is especially significant. For younger children, it needs to be the parent's responsibility to remind them to take their medications.

Most children and teenagers are very reluctant to go to the nurse's office in the middle of the day to take a medication. This needs to be taken into consideration when a medication decision is being made.

Remember that one of the most common reasons a medication is not helpful is that it was never taken.

RULE #20

Lack of effectiveness of a medication does not mean that the diagnosis is incorrect.

Jerry is a nine-year-old boy who was diagnosed with AD/HD, inattentive type, several months ago. His parents brought him in for a consultation because of increasing difficulties at school. After completing a psychiatric evaluation and gathering information from other sources, it was clear that his symptoms were consistent with a diagnosis of AD/HD. The family began implementing some new strategies at home that had some benefit. In addition, the school also instituted some changes to help Jerry. Despite these changes, Jerry continued to struggle with his schoolwork. A decision was finally made to initiate a medication trial.

Jerry tolerated a stimulant medication trial without any major adverse side effects. However, despite an adequate therapeutic dose, there was no benefit to the medication. The next step was to stop the first medication and initiate a second medication trial, with a different type of stimulant medication. Once again, Jerry tolerated the medication without any adverse effects, but did not receive any benefit, despite taking an adequate therapeutic dose. Both Jerry and his parents were becoming frustrated and wondered if we were treating the right problem. They were concerned that maybe Jerry didn't have AD/HD, but that there was something else we were missing.

This scenario, although very frustrating, is not that uncommon. In this situation, it was very important to reconsider Jerry's diagnosis of AD/HD. After further information-gathering and school observation, Jerry's difficulties were still consistent with a diagnosis of AD/HD. There was no evidence of any mood or anxiety disorders. Jerry also had neuropsychological testing done that showed no evidence of a learning disability. A speech and language evaluation was also done, but again, there was no evidence of any deficits. His presentation still appeared to be most consistent with AD/HD, inattentive type. It was decided to do a medication trial with a different type of medication. Once again, Jerry tolerated the medication well, except for a moderate decrease in his appetite. On this medication, Jerry did receive a moderate benefit.

There are some children and teenagers who do have AD/HD, but who do not receive any benefit from certain types of medications. It is important to try medication trials from the different classes of medications. In this case, it was also important to consider other potential diagnoses, such as mood or anxiety disorders.

Lack of effectiveness of a medication in the treatment of AD/HD doesn't mean that the AD/HD diagnosis is incorrect; however, in those situations it is essential to re-evaluate the entire situation. Part of that process might include getting a second opinion from a different physician. The majority of physicians favor getting consultations from their colleagues when it is necessary, and you shouldn't feel awkward requesting one.

RULE #21

Don't feel under pressure to make an urgent decision regarding the use of medications for your child.

Sarah is an 11-year-old girl who has been having a very difficult time with her schoolwork, as well as getting along with other children. Sarah's teacher expressed some concerns to Sarah's parents regarding her behavior and her ability to learn in the classroom. The teacher suggested that Sarah be evaluated for AD/HD and that perhaps the family should consider medications.

Sarah's father called me, in a panic, requesting a consultation. The family said this was an urgent situation, as Sarah's school was administering standardized exams the upcoming week, and Sarah was bound to do poorly unless something was done. The school also expressed concern that Sarah might not be promoted to the next grade.

Sarah's situation is a difficult one. Certainly there was some urgency to getting Sarah the proper help that she needed. Her parents were under a great deal of pressure from the school to do something right away. I explained to the parents that Sarah definitely did need a comprehensive diagnostic evaluation and that it would be important to evaluate for the presence of AD/HD, along with other potential causes of her current difficulties. From our conversation, it became clear that these concerns had been present for several years, but had become more severe over the last few months. I explained to them the necessity of the evaluation, prior to initiating any kind of treatment.

Emergency situations where an urgent decision needs to be made regarding initiating medication treatment for AD/HD are rare. As stated previously, it is of utmost value to have a comprehensive diagnostic evaluation prior to initiating any kind of treatment. This is even more important when medication treatment is being considered. In Sarah's situation, there was a possibility that she would have to repeat a grade. In situations like these, it is important to look at the "big picture" goals for Sarah.

If repeating a grade is seen as the worst possible outcome for Sarah, then naturally, certain treatment decisions will be made reflecting that premise. That is why it is important to look at the entire situation and all possible outcomes. For some children, repeating a grade has tremendous significance for both their long-term academic performance and their peer interactions.

Once the evaluation was completed, it was clear that Sarah did have AD/HD. It was also evident that she could potentially benefit from a medication trial. The urgent nature of the situation aided in the choice of medications, since some medications tend to show a potential benefit sooner than other medications.

Each child is unique and each situation is unique. It is important to thoroughly evaluate all of the different aspects that impact your child's life. You must look at both short-term and long-term goals.

As a parent, you should never feel you have to make a decision on the spot regarding the use of medications in the treatment of AD/HD (recall that this point was also discussed in Rule # 16 since it is an important point worth emphasizing).

SECTION 3—The Medications

There are two classes of medications currently in use for the treatment of AD/HD: ***stimulants and non-stimulants***.

Part 1: Stimulants

Introduction

- These medications have been around a long time. The behavioral effects of stimulants were accidentally discovered more than sixty years ago. Most experts still recommend them as the drugs of choice in the treatment of AD/HD. There have yet to be any other medicines to equal their potential benefit in the treatment of AD/HD.
- Most physicians have a great deal of experience with stimulants. They have been used in the treatment of AD/HD for more than 40 years. In addition, there have been more than 200 randomized controlled studies using stimulants. The majority of these studies included school-age children and teenagers. This huge body of research evidence provides a tremendous guide to the potential benefits, as well as the potential adverse effects, of this class of medication.
- Stimulants are classified as controlled substances (Schedule II) by the Drug Enforcement Agency because

they are amphetamines. This usually means that your doctor can write a prescription for only a limited amount (a one-month to three-month supply) without any refills. In addition, the physician usually cannot call in stimulant prescriptions to your local pharmacy, nor can he fax the prescription to your pharmacy. The pharmacy must receive an original, hard-copy prescription, with an original signature. Some states even require triplicate forms. You should check with the prescribing physician regarding your specific state laws.

- In certain people, stimulants may have some abuse potential. **However, most evidence to date indicates that there is no increased risk of abuse or addiction in those who take the medication for the treatment of AD/HD.** Actually, recent studies have demonstrated that the use of stimulant medications in the treatment of AD/HD **decreases the risk** of substance abuse. If, later on, the person develops a problem with substance abuse, it is most likely due to the AD/HD or other unrelated factors that contributed to their addiction. They are, however, contraindicated (not recommended) in those with a history of abuse of stimulants, unless there can be very close supervision of the administration of the medication. In those who have had a problem in the past with abusing other substances such as alcohol, marijuana, pain killers, benzodiazepines, etc., these medications are not contraindicated, but must be used with caution. Once again, there needs to be very close monitoring of the medications.
- Even though these medications are recommended as the drugs of choice in the treatment of AD/HD, their specific mechanism of action on the brain is not yet known. However, there are many potential theories that seem very plausible. It is known that the stimulants have some effects on the brain chemicals dopamine and norepinephrine. These chemicals are present in some

specific circuits in certain parts of the brain (especially the frontal lobe) that involve some of the functions that are impaired in AD/HD.

- Extreme caution should be used when stimulants are prescribed for children or teenagers with eating disorders, since there can be significant weight loss with the majority of these medications. This is another reason why a thorough diagnostic evaluation needs to be done prior to the initiation of any kind of treatment.
- There are several other contraindications to the use of stimulants. These include a prior allergic reaction, glaucoma, high blood pressure, hyperthyroidism, and cardiovascular disease.
- **Children and adolescents need to be monitored closely by a physician while on these medications.** There needs to be regular, face-to-face contact between your child or teenager and their prescribing physician. The physician needs to continually monitor how well your child is doing, as well as evaluate them for the presence of any adverse effects.

Potential Benefits

- Numerous double-blind placebo-controlled studies have demonstrated the effectiveness of stimulants in the treatment of AD/HD. This is the standard way in the field of medicine to determine if a certain treatment is legitimately effective.
- Research shows that the stimulant medications can possibly benefit the most prominent and function-impairing symptoms of AD/HD. There is a purported increase in focus and concentration, as well as a decrease in distractibility. Also noted is a decrease in impulsivity and aggression. As a result, there is a potential benefit in improved classroom behavior and academic performance, as well as in interactions with peers and adults. The research studies ranged in duration from

less than three months up to 24 months. Moreover, throughout the two years of treatment, it appeared that the stimulant medication continued to be effective in the treatment of AD/HD symptoms.

- Approximately 70–75% of children will have a beneficial response from the stimulants. **Each child or teenager will have a unique response to the medications.** The benefits to one teenager could be more, or less, as compared to another teenager on the same medication. The medications are not likely to normalize all of the difficulties. However, there are some situations where certain children and teenagers, while on the medication, will function as non-AD/HD children. In numerous instances, the advantages seen on the medications are only present when the medications are taken. In other words, if the medications were to be stopped, the benefits that were evident during medication treatment would cease.
- **Stimulants are the definite drugs of choice when an immediate benefit is needed.**

Potential Adverse Effects

- The majority of side effects that occur do not warrant stopping the medication. It will be important to consult with the prescribing physician prior to stopping a medication due to an adverse effect.
- The most common potential side effects are:

  1) Abdominal pain and headaches

  - Taking the medicines with food or right after breakfast can help alleviate some of the discomfort. These two side effects tend to decrease with time once the body has adjusted to being on the medicine.
  - It is important to remember that both abdominal pain and headaches are common complaints among school-age children, as well as some teenagers.

2) **These medications tend to consistently lower the appetite.**
   - For some children and teenagers, the decrease in appetite can be a gauge of how effective the dosing is. If, during treatment, the appetite begins to increase, it is possible that the medicine is losing some of its benefit. Ask your child about the actual amount of food they are eating at lunch while at school. Sometimes it is a good idea to consult their teacher if your child is not able to accurately report how much they are eating. **There needs to be regular weight monitoring.**
   - Foods that are high in calories can help make up some of the weight loss. There are many high-calorie nutritious shakes currently available on the market.
   - When the longer-acting stimulants wear off, there tends to be an increase in appetite later in the day, around bedtime. As a result, sometimes there is a need to push dinner to a later time so the medication can get out of the system.
3) **All stimulants have the potential to cause insomnia.**
   - The longer-acting medicines tend to have a higher risk because they remain in the system longer.
   - It is important to note your child or teenager's baseline sleep pattern prior to initiating the medication, since ***it is sometimes difficult to differentiate difficulty settling for bed (a common experience for people with AD/HD) from insomnia.***
   - A difficult decision arises when the medicine is working well and is well-tolerated, except for the insomnia, since a restful night's sleep is very important for anyone's function. This is especially true for children and adolescents. **Sometimes over-the-counter sleep aids, such as Melatonin, can be helpful.** (There is no current published

data on the benefit of Melatonin to treat insomnia in children or teenagers, but there are many physicians who have found it clinically helpful for their patients.) You will need to check with your physician or pharmacist regarding how much to give. In this situation, the benefit of the medication has to outweigh the risk of using a medication for sleep.

4) **Sometimes when the stimulants are given in a higher dose, they can cause "over-focusing."**
    - Over-focusing is when an individual gets stuck on what they are doing, and cannot disengage from the task, resulting in difficulty transitioning to another activity.
    - Children with obsessive-compulsive tendencies and rigid, inflexible personalities tend to be especially vulnerable to this effect.
    - Lowering the dose or stopping the medicine should alleviate the problem if the "over-focusing" is, in fact, caused by the prescribed medication.
5) **Another potential adverse effect of a high dose is a flattening of the affect, where the child looks like he has no facial expression and looks "drugged."**
    - ***This is important to differentiate from depression.*** Lowering the dose or stopping the medicine should result in a return to a regular facial expression. In this case, the benefit of the medication probably does not outweigh this adverse effect, but this needs to be evaluated on an individual basis, taking into account your child or teenager's unique situation and needs.
6) **Disturbances in growth**
    - Some studies have shown a reduction in the rate of a child's growth when stimulants are actively being taken. However, there does appear to be a rebound in the rate of growth once the medications are discontinued, and there appears to

be no ultimate discrepancy in the height attained. **There is still a need to monitor the growth curve with your child's pediatrician.** There is also the option of not giving the medications on weekends or holidays, if this becomes a major concern. If not giving the medication is not a viable option, sometimes giving a lower dose of the medication is a good alternative. If growth suppression continues to be a problem, it is reasonable to try either a different stimulant medication, or a non-stimulant medication as an alternative.

7) **There can be a mild increase in heart rate and blood pressure.**
   - For the majority of children, this is not clinically significant. The American Heart Association **does not** currently recommend obtaining an EKG prior to the initiation of stimulant medications.
   - If your child has a structural cardiac abnormality or a history of increased heart rate or blood pressure, then caution must be taken in the use of stimulants. An EKG is warranted before treatment is initiated, and again several weeks after the medication is started.

   If there is a family history of sudden death or premature cardiac disease, a more thorough cardiac evaluation must be performed before stimulant medications are considered. If your child or teenager is adopted and a family history is not available, it is prudent to get an EKG prior to the initiation of treatment, as well as after the stimulant medication has been started.

8) **As the medication is wearing off, there can be "rebound effects":**
   - Increased AD/HD symptoms
   - Increased emotional sensitivity
   - Moodiness and irritability
   - Fatigue

These effects can be very troubling and significant. **If they occur when a long-acting stimulant is wearing off, adding a short-acting stimulant at a low dose may help alleviate the problem.** The primary risk of that strategy is an increased potential for insomnia.

9) **Other potential adverse effects include:**
   - The presence of moodiness and irritability. This can be confirmed if there is a decrease in these symptoms when the medications are not given. The risk is increased if there is an underlying mood disorder such as major depression or bipolar disorder. It is important to remember that children and adolescents with AD/HD have an increased amount of moodiness and irritability at baseline.
   - The presence of anxiety symptoms such as picking at the skin or nail biting. Similar to underlying depression, this is especially common in children and adolescents who already suffer from anxiety disorders, such as separation anxiety disorder or obsessive-compulsive disorder. Increased anxiety often manifests as clinginess in young children.
   - It will be important to determine if these symptoms are present while the medicine is in full effect, or if these symptoms are only present as the medicine is wearing off each day (indicating a rebound effect—see above).
   - On **very rare** occasions, some children have hallucinations or paranoia on high doses.
   - **In children who might have an underlying tic disorder, the medications can precipitate an increase.** This doesn't mean that stimulants cannot be used in children who have an underlying tic disorder, but they should be used with caution. Research studies have shown that the stimulants **do not cause** tic disorders such as Tourette's syndrome.

Current Available Stimulants

All stimulant medications have the same potential benefit and the same potential set of adverse effects. They tend to differ with respect to how long it takes for them to begin working, as well as how long they remain effective during a given day. The three categories are: Long-Acting Preparations, Intermediate Acting Preparations, and Short-Acting Preparations. The duration of action of a given stimulant can potentially have an impact on the occurrence of adverse effects. As with any other medications, each individual will respond uniquely to a given stimulant. It is not uncommon for a specific medication to last twelve hours in one person, and six hours in another. There are also situations where a child or teenager can have a beneficial response to one stimulant, but not to the others.

There are three different kinds of stimulants that are currently used in the treatment of AD/HD:

1) ***Methylphenidate*** (Brand Names: Ritalin, Focalin, Methylin, Ritalin LA, Ritalin SR, Metadate CD, Concerta, Focalin XR)
2) ***Dextroamphetamine*** (Brand Names: Dexedrine, Dextrostat, Dexedrine Spansules)
3) ***Dextroamphetamine and racemic amphetamine*** (Brand Names: Adderall, Adderall XR)

Current Available Long-Acting Preparations

1) **Adderall XR**—The capsule can be opened up and sprinkled on food for children who cannot swallow pills. 50% of the active medication is released immediately; the remaining 50% is released four to six hours later. Because of the higher percentage of immediate release medication, there is a potential increased benefit during the first one to two hours after the medication is given. Adderall XR is currently available in 5mg, 10mg, 15mg, 20mg, 25mg, and 30mg capsules. The six available strengths provide a great deal of flexibility in dosing Adderall XR.

2) **Concerta**—The outer shell of the capsule contains active medication, so it cannot be opened or cut. 22% of the active medication is on the outer shell and is released immediately; 78% is released continuously and produces increasing concentrations of active medication. Concerta may potentially provide better effectiveness at the end of the day in comparison to the other methylphenidate preparations. There is usually a need to increase the Concerta dose in order to see more of a benefit during the first two hours after the medication has been given. An additional benefit of Concerta is that its outer coat cannot be tampered with so there is limited potential for abuse. Concerta is currently available in 18mg, 27mg, 36mg, and 54mg capsules. The current approved maximum dosage is 72mg a day.
3) **Focalin XR**—This drug is the most recently approved by the FDA for the treatment of AD/HD in children, adolescents, and adults. Both Focalin XR and the short-acting preparation Focalin are actually dexmethylphenidate (d-MPH) compounds (a pharmacological variation of the methylphenidate molecule that makes it more pharmacologically active). Similar to Adderall XR and Concerta, Focalin XR is a medication taken once in the morning, with the potential benefit of 12 hours of effectiveness. Focalin XR offers an important variation from Concerta, in that 50% of the dose is released immediately, and the remaining 50% is released several hours later. As a result, there is a potentially increased benefit during the first several hours after the medication is given. An additional feature of Focalin XR is that it can be taken whole, or the contents of the capsule can be sprinkled on food. Focalin XR is currently available in 3 dosage strengths: 5mg, 10mg, and 20mg capsules.

All three long-acting preparations can potentially remain effective for up to 12 hours after the morning dose is taken. All three preparations have the same potential benefit and the same potential adverse effects with only minor differences between the three during treatment. There are currently no published studies that compare any of the three long-acting preparations. These long-acting preparations are ideal for use throughout the day, so there is no need for trips to the school nurse to receive medications. An added benefit of the long-acting formulations is increased adherence, which means fewer medications to remember. In some children, the medication effectiveness runs out either before, or during homework time, and there is a need for a low dose of a short-acting preparation. The main concern with that strategy is an increased risk for insomnia, and a potential for further inhibition of the appetite during dinnertime.

The Most Commonly Used Available Intermediate-Acting Preparations

1) **Metadate CD**—This medication can have a potential duration of action of up to 8 hours. It comes in capsule form, which can be opened up and the beads sprinkled on food. 30% of the medication is released immediately; 70% is released continuously. Metadate CD tends to have a fast onset of action (within 1.5 hours of taking the dose). Metadate CD is available in 10mg, 20mg, and 30mg capsules.
2) **Ritalin LA**—Similar to the Metadate CD, it can last up to 8 hours and comes in capsule form that contains beads which can be sprinkled on food. The difference is that 50% of the medication is released immediately while the remaining 50% is released four hours later. Because 50% is released immediately, there is a greater potential benefit during the first several hours, as compared to other methylphenidate preparations. Ritalin LA is available in 10mg, 20mg, 30mg, and 40mg capsules.
3) **Dexedrine Spansules**—Its duration of effectiveness can potentially last from 5 to 8 hours. There is an immediate release of an initial dose, then a second release of the

rest of the medication. Dexedrine Spansules is available in 5mg, 10mg, and 15mg capsules. It is currently available in generic form.

These intermediate-acting preparations are ideal for children or teenagers who only need the medication during the school day, and not during after-school activities. In some instances where these preparations are only effective for 6 hours, they can be used twice a day if needed. There are other intermediate-acting preparations also available that are not currently commonly used. These preparations include: Ritalin SR, Metadate ER, and Methylin ER.

Current Available Short-Acting Preparations

1) **Adderall**—can last 4–6 hours
2) **Ritalin, Focalin, Dextrostat**—can last 3–5 hours
3) **Methylin**—is now available as an oral solution and as sprinkles, which is an important feature for younger children who cannot swallow pills.

These short-acting preparations are ideal for use in several different situations. A common current use is during the early evening hours. This tends to occur especially after the long-acting or intermediate-acting preparations' effects have run out. As mentioned earlier, giving a short-acting preparation during the early evening hours can increase the risk for insomnia. Another potential setting for using a short-acting preparation is during weekends or holidays when your child does not take their long-acting or intermediate-acting preparations, but needs to focus or concentrate for a specific time-limited activity.

A less common situation when the short-acting preparations are needed is when a child needs to take a stimulant as soon as he wakes up because the AD/HD symptoms are severe, and he is not able to function during the morning routine before the long-acting stimulant has time to kick in. This tends to occur more frequently with Concerta, because only a small percentage of the medication is released immediately. There are some children and teen-agers who experience more adverse effects when the long-acting or intermediate-acting preparations are taken. In those cases, the short-acting preparations are given either three or four times a day, depending on the duration of action in the given individual. In these instances, the child or teenager will have to go to the school nurse to get their mid-school-day dose. It will be imperative to closely monitor how long each dose of medication is effective, so the next dose can be given before the effectiveness of the previous dose has worn off.

What to expect during treatment

Prior to initiating the medications, it is worthwhile to have different AD/HD scales (standardized evaluation forms used to measure the severity and frequency of AD/HD symptoms) completed by a caregiver, as well as by several teachers. Once the medication is started, your child must be monitored regularly by a physician to assure that the medication is working, and that your child is not experiencing any adverse effects.

There are two different approaches to starting stimulant treatment:

1) The first approach involves beginning treatment with a short-acting stimulant and adjusting the dosage until the correct amount can be determined. Once the total amount has been determined, then there is a switch to the equivalent long-acting medication.

Approximate equivalents:

A) Concerta:

18mg = 5mg methylphenidate three times a day
27mg = 7.5mg methylphenidate three times a day
36mg = 10mg methylphenidate three times a day
54mg = 15mg methylphenidate three times a day

B) Focalin XR:

5mg = 2.5 mg Focalin twice a day
10mg = 5mg Focalin twice a day
20mg = 10mg Focalin twice a day

C) Adderall XR:

Long-acting dose is equivalent to the short-acting dose given twice a day. For example, 10mg of Adderall XR is equal to 5mg of regular Adderall, given twice a day.

D) Ritalin LA and Metadate CD:

Intermediate acting dose is equivalent to the short-acting dose given twice a day.

2) The second approach involves initiating treatment with a long-acting medication. It is generally a good principle to start with the smallest dose. Once it is clear the medication has been tolerated, the dose can be increased.

Regardless of which approach is used, the child should be monitored at all times to determine if there is any benefit to the different dosages, and of course, if the medication was tolerated. As stated previously, most adverse events, such as headaches and abdominal pain, tend to be transient. However, if an unacceptable adverse effect persists, it is reasonable to consult with the prescribing physician regarding stopping the medication trial.

At times, there is a correlation between the amount of the dosage and the duration of action of the medication. Sometimes, when the amount is increased, the medication can last longer. If a medication is clearly helping, but there is still a need for improvement, you should consult the physician regarding a possible increase in dose.

There are some instances when there is a frequent need to increase the dose of the medication. Some children and teenagers develop tolerance to the benefits of the medication rather quickly, so the medication is no longer effective. It is important to remember that children and teenagers are still growing, so they tend to adjust to medications much more quickly and more frequently than adults do. This is especially true during early- and mid-adolescence when most growth spurts occur.

Many people ask how long their child should remain on the stimulant medication. This question needs to be answered on an individual basis. There are times when the medications are just not worth it; the benefit is unclear, or the adverse effects are too many, or both. Regardless, it still must be determined on an individual basis. One factor is the severity of the symptoms. The less impaired someone is, the less need for the medications. Another issue is how well the child has learned other tools to compensate for the AD/HD symptoms. Other aspects include change of environment or change of academic expectations. ***It is important to remember that a significant number of children and adolescents continue to have significant AD/HD symptoms into adulthood and continue to benefit from the use of medications.***

Part 2: Non-Stimulants

Atomoxetine (Strattera)

Introduction

- Strattera is the first **non-stimulant** medication that has been FDA-approved for the treatment of AD/HD in children, adolescents and adults. Strattera has only been available in the United States since November 2002. Even though it is not a scheduled medication and has no abuse or dependence potential, this medication still requires a prescription. This means that the prescribing physician can write refills on the prescriptions, and can call in or fax the prescription to your local pharmacy. Its mechanism of action is as a selective norepinephrine reuptake inhibitor. It has currently not been tested or approved for use in children less than 6 years of age.
- There are clear differences between Strattera and the stimulants regarding treatment and potential adverse events. An adequate trial of Strattera requires at least 3–5 weeks on a therapeutic dose, whereas the benefits of the stimulants are evident much sooner. So a clear distinction is that the stimulants potentially have a much quicker onset of action, and results may be evident when the medication trial is first initiated.
- The benefits of Strattera tend to be more subtle than the stimulants, and at times, Strattera might appear to

not be as effective. This is especially true for children or teenagers who have been effectively treated with the stimulant medications. Most people on stimulants can tell when the medication begins to work and when it wears off. This is not always the case with Strattera.

- Strattera needs to be taken on a daily basis, whereas with the stimulants, a day or two can be skipped (for example, over the weekend). Moreover, the stimulants only work on the days that they are taken, and there is no carryover into the next day. Strattera is currently available in 10mg, 18mg, 25mg, 40mg, and 60mg capsules. These capsules cannot be opened up and sprinkled.

How is Strattera dosed?

- Strattera can be given either once or twice a day. This is best determined by the response to the medication. It is possible to take it either in the evening, in the morning, or both. Your child's physician can help you make those decisions. As previously stated several times, each person's response to any medication is unique. Since fatigue or tiredness can be a side effect of Straterra, it is usually best to start Strattera in the evening for 10–14 days before switching it to the morning.
- The dosing for Strattera is usually determined by weight. It is prudent to initiate the medication on a low dose for a few days, just to make sure there are no unexpected adverse effects. The current total daily maximum dosing is 1.2–1.5 mg/kg/day. In many instances, the medication can be effective without necessarily needing the maximum dose.

Potential Benefits

- According to the FDA-approved studies done by Eli Lilly (the maker of Strattera), Strattera was found to be effective in the treatment of all AD/HD symptoms. Strattera also tends to have less of a propensity to increase anxiety or cause mood disturbances in comparison to the stimulants. In fact, in two recent studies, Strattera was shown to decrease anxiety in children and adolescents with AD/HD. In adolescents who have had difficulties with substance abuse, Strattera would be a reasonable choice, since it does not appear to have any abuse potential. There is also a lower of risk for insomnia on Strattera.

- A potential benefit of Strattera is that, when effective, it can alleviate AD/HD symptoms throughout the entire day. This is especially beneficial in the evenings when the stimulant medication has worn off, or early in the morning, when the stimulant has yet to kick in.

Potential Adverse Effects

- As with any other medication, Strattera does have some potential negative effects. Most of the side effects that are experienced tend to be minimal and do not result in the medication having to be stopped. **However, this is a decision that needs to be made on an individual basis.**
- If your child does experience a side effect, you, along with your physician, must decide if the benefit of the medicine outweighs the side effects. It is always good to remember that most side effects tend to subside within a week.
- The most common side effects that are experienced:

  1) **Stomach upset**
     - As with any other medication, to minimize stomach upset, Strattera can be taken with food.

  2) **Tiredness**
     - If your child experiences tiredness when the Strattera is given in the morning, it would be reasonable to consider switching it to the evening. Keep in mind, however, that whenever the medication is switched to the evening, there is always the possibility that the medication will be less effective.

- Another reasonable approach would be to give some in the morning, and some in the evening. Once again, this can cause a difference in how well the medication is working, but at times there can be an increase in benefit by taking the medication twice a day, because the potential benefit of the medication can be evenly split throughout the day.

3) **Weight loss as a result of decreased appetite**
   - The degree of weight loss tends to be less than experienced with the stimulants. Similar to the stimulant medications, growth needs to be monitored during treatment.
4) **Increased blood pressure and heart rate**
   - If your child has a cardiac condition, you must alert your physician to this prior to the initiation of the Strattera trial. For the majority of children, this increase in heart rate and blood pressure is not clinically significant.
5) **Other potential adverse effects:**
   - Nausea or vomiting
   - Dizziness
   - Dry mouth
   - Diarrhea or constipation
   - Agitation and irritability at high doses

In December of 2004, the FDA issued a warning on Strattera:

Out of two million people, there were two reported cases of liver injury that were both reversible. One case was that of an adult, and the other was an adolescent. There is no current recommendation for doing routine blood monitoring of the liver. However, it is important to discuss with your child's physician some of the signs of liver disease, such as yellowing of the skin, itching, dark urine, unexplained "flu-like" symptoms, etc. Since there have only been two cases reported (as of publication), it is difficult to establish a cause and effect relationship to Strattera. However, since Strattera has only been on the market for a few years, it might be wise to check blood monitoring of the liver from time to time. As mentioned before, there are no current recommendations regarding the frequency that this should be done.

Strattera Label Change: September 2005

In conjunction with a request from the US Food and Drug Administration, Eli Lilly agreed to put a warning on Strattera because of possible uncommon reports of suicidal thoughts among children and adolescents. The Strattera clinical trials database identified 5 cases out of 1357 patients (0.4%) who had suicidal thoughts. ***As of publication, there have been no reported suicides among children, adolescents, or adults on the medication.***

These two warnings emphasize the need for monitoring by a physician any child or adolescent who is taking any medication for the treatment of AD/HD.

What to expect during treatment

- Strattera must be taken daily. It is better to start at a low dose, and then increase the dose to a therapeutic level, once tolerability has been established.
- A possible side effect of increasing the dose is **irritability and moodiness**. As stated previously, this tends to occur on the higher dosage levels.
- As with the stimulants, your child or teenager needs to be monitored by a physician during treatment. It is always valuable to continue to reassess the benefit of the medication versus whatever negative effects are present.

Combination treatment of Atomoxetine (Strattera) with stimulants

- The decision to initiate a medication trial is a difficult one. The decision to combine two medications needs to be evaluated in the same manner. The same medication "rules" are in effect. The same variables need to be evaluated:

- Goal of treatment
- Potential benefit versus potential risk
- The risk of not treating

When should this option be considered?

- The potential for combining Atomoxetine with a stimulant arises when one of the medications has only a partial benefit. Before combination treatment is considered, it is generally more prudent to stop the medication with the partial benefit and initiate a second medication trial with a medication that has yet to be tried.
- Combination treatment might be indicated if all of the different medications that are well-tolerated only have a partial benefit.

Potential risks

- The main risk to be aware of is the increased potential for adverse effects when medications are combined. There will also be a higher risk for a decrease in appetite, since both the stimulants and Atomoxetine can lower the appetite.
- There will also be a need to monitor blood pressure and heart rate, since both medications can potentially increase both heart rate and blood pressure.
- Another potential negative effect is an increased risk for the nuisance side effects, such as stomach upset, headaches, dizziness, nausea, vomiting, dry mouth, etc.
- Another aspect to consider with combination treatment is that many children don't like the idea of taking more than one medication. This is especially true of some adolescents who have

mixed feelings about being on the medication in the first place.

Important point to consider regarding combination treatment

- It is important to note that there is currently limited data on combining Atomoxetine with stimulant medications, although it has become a common practice. There are currently more studies underway to examine the safety and efficacy of this combination.

Bupropion (Wellbutrin)

Introduction

- Bupropion is primarily an antidepressant that is sometimes used in the treatment of AD/HD. Bupropion affects the same chemicals (dopamine and norepinephrine) as the other AD/HD drugs.
- Bupropion is currently available as a once-a-day medication in the Wellbutrin XL form; twice-a-day in the Wellbutrin SR form; and three-times-a-day in the Wellbutrin (non-extended release) form. Bupropion is also currently available in generic form.

Several studies have shown that Bupropion can have a potential benefit in improving both AD/HD symptoms and depression.

- One of these studies showed Bupropion to be superior to placebo (sugar pill) in the treatment of childhood AD/HD. However, the benefit seen was less than that seen with the stimulants. Many of the studies conducted to date have had small numbers of people enrolled, so there is a clear need for more research.

Potential Benefits

- Bupropion would be a good option for the treatment of AD/HD in the existence of depression, or in those who are at risk for bipolar disorder. Bupropion would also be an ideal alternative in an adolescent who has a history of substance abuse, where stimulants could cause a potential complication.
- **In children or adolescents who received no benefit from or could not tolerate either Strattera or the stimulants, a Wellbutrin trial could be the next logical choice.**
- In children or adolescents who have lost a great deal of weight on some of the other medications, a Bupropion trial would also be the next logical choice since Bupropion's impact on weight is significantly less than the stimulants or Strattera.
- Currently, there is no need for routine blood tests or Electrocardiograms (ECGs).

Potential adverse effects

- There can be increased difficulty falling asleep, as well as a potential increased risk of agitation and anxiety.
- Wellbutrin is contraindicated in the presence of eating disorders as well as seizure disorders due to the possible increased risk of seizures at high doses.

What to expect during treatment

- Wellbutrin XL should be taken with food in the morning. The later in the day it is taken, the higher the risk for trouble falling asleep.
- **Wellbutrin will potentially take several weeks to work.** A medication trial at an adequate dosage should be at least six weeks, unless the Wellbutrin is not tolerated.
- The overall potential benefit in the treatment of AD/HD is less than the stimulants.

Alpha-Blockers: Clonidine (Catapres) and Guanfacine (Tenex)

Introduction

- There are two medications available in this class:
    - Clonidine (Catapres)
    - Guanfacine (Tenex)
- Both of these medications were initially designed to treat high blood pressure.
    - They tend to be used in combination with other AD/HD medications. There is some research data that shows they are beneficial as solo agents, but clinically, they tend to be used in combination with other AD/HD medications.

Potential benefit

- The main potential benefit is their ability to decrease levels of impulsivity, hyperactivity and aggression; however, their benefit in helping inattention, distractibility, and executive dysfunction appears to be limited.
- **Alpha-Blockers are a good choice in children and adolescents with tics, because they are routinely used in the treatment of tic disorders, such as Tourette's syndrome.** Several studies have shown the combination of Clonidine and methylphenidate to be effective in the treatment of both AD/HD and tic disorder symptoms. Guanfacine has also been shown to be effective in the treatment of AD/HD symptoms and tics, but the beneficial effect on AD/HD symptoms was less than that of the stimulants.
- **Alpha-Blockers can also potentially promote the onset of sleep, especially when a stimulant is also being taken.**
- If necessary, they can be prescribed in the evening to potentially alleviate the morning symptoms (before the onset of action of the stimulant).

Potential adverse effects

- Alpha-Blockers can cause some potential adverse effects that are a product of the manner in which they work on the brain, as well as their potential to lower blood pressure. These potential negative effects can include:
  1) Dizziness
  2) Sedation
  3) Fatigue
  4) Light-headedness
  5) A potential rebound increase in blood pressure, if a dose is missed.
  6) There is also the possibility of an actual decrease in blood pressure.
- **These medications are contraindicated in the presence of significant cardiac disease.** There have been several reports of cardiovascular adverse effects in patients taking Clonidine for the treatment of AD/HD.
- There have also been some concerns about a possible worsening of depressive symptoms on Clonidine.

What to expect during treatment

- It is sensible to do an ECG prior to treatment and after treatment has been initiated. This is a must if either Clonidine or Guanfacine are going to be combined with a stimulant medication. There have been four reported instances of sudden death in patients who were taking both methylphenidate and Clonidine.
- Periodic blood pressure checks are necessary.
- **Because of the possible rebound increase in blood pressure, Clonidine and Guanfacine need to be tapered down gradually if they are going to be discontinued.**
- Clonidine is available as a patch that delivers the medication over a twenty-four hour period. The difficulty with this delivery system is that it tends to fall off frequently or can get pulled off by either your child or another child.

Modafinil (Provigil)

- Modafinil is a medication that is currently approved for the treatment of narcolepsy and excessive daytime sedation.
- There have been several trials in children that have examined its potential benefit in the treatment of AD/HD. Most of these trials enrolled a small number of children.
- Some of these trials did show a potential benefit in the treatment of AD/HD, but the results have been mixed. At this time, there is inadequate data and experience on the use of Modafinil in the treatment of AD/HD.
- Modafinil could have the same potential adverse effects as the traditional stimulants, except that it seems less likely to lower the appetite.

Tricyclic Antidepressants (TCAs)

Introduction

- Tricyclic antidepressants have been used for many years in the treatment of depression in adults. There is currently no reliable research data showing that they are effective as antidepressants in children.
- TCAs have been used in the treatment of children and adolescents diagnosed with AD/HD who have not responded to or who could not tolerate the stimulants.
- Some of the TCAs that have been used in the treatment of AD/HD include Desipramine, Imipramine, and Nortriptyline.

Potential benefits

- There is much data showing that these antidepressants are effective in the treatment of AD/HD. Several of these studies have shown them to be superior to placebo in the treatment of AD/HD. The majority of the studies do show that the stimulants are usually equal or superior in their potential benefit in the treatment of AD/HD.

- The TCAs can be useful in certain children and adolescents who suffer from both AD/HD and a tic disorder. Desipramine was shown to be effective in reducing both the tic and AD/HD symptoms in comparison to placebo.

Potential adverse effects

- Despite having a known benefit in the treatment of AD/HD, caution needs to be used when considering these drugs. This class of medications has many adverse effects that require close monitoring.
- The major adverse event that makes the TCAs a medication of last resort is the **potential for cardiac toxicity.**
  - There are several reported cases of sudden death that have been reported in children taking Tricyclic antidepressants. Five of the sudden deaths occurred in children taking Desipramine.
  - Children who are put on these medications need close cardiac monitoring—especially the measurement of the QTc interval prior to the initiation of the medication, and subsequent to each increase in dose. There are other potential ECG changes that also need to be monitored.
- Other adverse effects specific to these medications:
  1) Drowsiness
  2) Increased risk for seizures
  3) Confusion
  4) Dry mouth
  5) Blurred vision
  6) Constipation

Potential benefits versus potential risks

- **Due to the potential cardiac risks and the other potential adverse effects, there are generally few situations where the potential benefit of these**

medications in the treatment of AD/HD outweighs the potential negative risks.

- Since there are some children who cannot tolerate the stimulants and who receive little benefit from the other options, these medications can be an option with **close monitoring and consultation with your child or teenager's physician.**

Venlafaxine (Effexor)

- Venlafaxine is a serotonin/norepinephrine reuptake inhibitor that is FDA-approved for the treatment of depression and anxiety in adults. There have been several trials conducted in children and adolescents to evaluate its effectiveness in the treatment of AD/HD. The number of children and adolescents enrolled in these trials has been inadequate. **At this time, the results seem to be inconclusive regarding its potential benefit in the treatment of AD/HD.**

Potential adverse effects

- Activation
  - Venlafaxine can potentially exacerbate AD/HD symptoms, resulting in an increase in hyperactivity, impulsivity, and distractibility.
- Other potential adverse events:
  1) Sleepiness and fatigue
  2) Gastrointestinal: nausea, vomiting, diarrhea, or abdominal pain
  3) Headaches
  4) Difficulty falling asleep or disrupted sleep
  5) There can be difficulties in stopping the medication; this needs to be done gradually due to the following potential withdrawal symptoms:
     - Headaches
     - Fatigue

- Increased sweating
- Nausea and vomiting
- Feeling jittery and agitated

Potential benefits versus potential risks

- **Because of the potential activation and the limited data on its effectiveness, Venlafaxine should be tried only if most of the other options have failed.**

SECTION 4—Q&A

General

Q: My child is fidgety and has a hard time sitting still. Should we try some Ritalin to see if it helps?

A: It is important to remember that not every child who fidgets or has a hard time sitting actually has AD/HD. It is paramount to first have your child evaluated. There is no reason to start a medication without knowing what you are treating; you need to know the diagnosis. It is possible that his symptoms are within normal behavior for his age, or are secondary to something else, like anxiety or an underlying medical disorder. Doing a medication trial with Ritalin is not a good way to determine if a child has a diagnosis of AD/HD. See Medication Rule #1.

Q: I have two boys. My older son was diagnosed with AD/HD. Should I be concerned that my younger son may also have it?

A: Your older son having AD/HD does not necessarily mean that the younger one will have it. However, since there is a family history, he is certainly at a higher risk. There are numerous studies that show that there is a genetic component to AD/HD, and that it does run in some families. Still, there is no reason to have your younger son evaluated unless he is exhibiting symptoms consistent with AD/HD.

Q: My child is not hyper, but his doctor thinks he has AD/HD. How could this be?

A: A person doesn't have to be hyper to have AD/HD. There are different subtypes of AD/HD. Some people have the predominantly hyperactive/impulsive kind, some have more of the inattention symptoms, and others have a combination of the two. You should still ask your child's doctor how he/she came to that diagnostic conclusion. You should also review the diagnostic criteria. Refer to Section 1, Part 2.

Q: My child has AD/HD. What kind of professional can prescribe medications?

A: In most states, only a physician is allowed to prescribe the medications; in some states, other professionals including physician assistants and nurse practitioners are also allowed to prescribe medications. Most pediatricians are comfortable treating AD/HD. If there are other difficulties such as anxiety or depression, it might be more beneficial to see a child & adolescent psychiatrist. These types of doctors specialize in seeing children and adolescents with emotional and behavioral difficulties. Refer to the American Academy of Child and Adolescent Psychiatry website (www.aacap.org) for a list of providers in your area, or ask your pediatrician for a referral. Pediatric neurologists and behavioral pediatricians are also specialists who treat AD/HD.

Q: My child is really struggling with her behavior and academics. Her teachers have been concerned for the last two years that she might have AD/HD, but I am against medications. What should we do?

A: The first thing you need to do is to get her evaluated. It will be very difficult to get your daughter help without knowing what you are treating. If, in fact, she does have AD/HD, there are some non-medication interventions that can be very beneficial. Even if you were to start her on a medication trial, it would still be helpful to utilize some of these non-medication strategies. You should also tell your child's physician why you are against medications. It is possible that some of your reasons are based on misinformation or prior negative experiences. If your child does have AD/HD, you will have to make a decision regarding medication treatment at some point. You can always get a second opinion regarding the diagnosis, as well the possible use of medications. As with all possible types of treatments being considered, you need to weigh the potential benefit of treatment versus the potential adverse effects. In addition, you need to factor in the potential negative consequences of choosing not to treat.

Q: We are thinking of starting my teenager on a medication trial for AD/HD. Should we tell her school?

A: This is a very difficult question to answer because each situation is unique. If your teenager is going to get her medication at school, then you will have to fill out a form signed by her doctor giving the school permission to administer the medication in the prescribed fashion. If you are going to start with a longer-acting medication that doesn't need to be administered at school, then you need to weigh the benefit versus the risk of telling the school. Most schools prefer to know when their students are on any medications. In case of a medical emergency, it is essential to know what medications the student is on. In addition, her teachers can potentially be helpful in monitoring your teenager's progress while she is on the medication.

There are situations when both parents and teenagers feel that if a student is on medication, they are somehow treated differently by the school. I have come across certain situations when teachers have made inappropriate comments to students regarding their use of the medications. Not all teachers have the same knowledge base or experience regarding AD/HD and its treatment. In some instances, you will need to educate the teachers and advocate on behalf of your teenager.

Q: Can you do a brain scan to diagnose AD/HD?

A: There are numerous brain scan methods that are used in AD/HD research. These include positron emission tomography (PET), single photon emission computed tomography (SPECT), and functional magnetic resonance imaging (fMRI). In research studies, AD/HD children have shown smaller brain volumes in specific parts of the brain—frontal lobes, white matter, and cerebellum. It is important to keep in mind that these are research study results only that reflect a group of AD/HD children. These scans remain only research tools, and cannot and should not be used to diagnose AD/HD in a specific child or teenager.

Medication Treatment

Q: My son has been diagnosed with AD/HD. His doctor tried him on Concerta. There was a moderate benefit, but he got headaches in the middle of the afternoon. Will the same thing happen if we try Adderall?

A: The occurrence of an adverse effect on one stimulant doesn't necessarily mean it will occur on another stimulant. It is standard practice to try a medication trial of a different stimulant even though there is still some risk for the same side effect.

Q: My twelve-year-old son has been doing well on Concerta for three years with no adverse effects. How long does he need to be on the medication?

A: The answer to this question will depend on your son's specific circumstances. There is no standard time frame for how long someone needs to stay on the medication. To best answer this question, there are several critical aspects that need to be assessed.

The first aspect is the existence of any adverse effects. In this case, there do not appear to be any adverse effects, so there is no urgent to reason to stop the medication. If there were adverse effects, then, in discussion with your child's physician, you would have to evaluate the current benefit of the medication versus the current adverse effects. The benefit would have to outweigh the adverse effects to be worthwhile.

A second aspect is how well your child has learned other strategies and skills to compensate for his difficulties. Every child is unique and has differing amounts of struggles secondary to their AD/HD symptoms. The extent of the skills that your son has learned to compensate for these symptoms needs to be taken into account in this decision.

A third aspect to bear in mind is that it is imperative to constantly re-evaluate the need for the medication. Sometimes there is a benefit to doing a trial off the medication. The only true trial will be during the school year since you will get a much more accurate picture of how well things go off the medication. Based on how well your child does off the medication, you can get an accurate picture of how things will be when you stop the medication.

There are numerous instances when many children and teenagers continue to need medication treatment into adulthood, but this is something that needs to be continually reevaluated.

Q: Will the medication make my teenager "look like a zombie?"

A: When a medication trial is initiated, there are two variables that are being evaluated: the effectiveness of the medication and the presence of any adverse effects. If you put your teenager on a medication that makes them "look like a zombie" then, assuming the medication is effective, the dose should be lowered. If that doesn't eliminate the problem, or if the medication is ineffective at the lower dose, then that medication needs to be stopped; if there is still a need for treatment, a different medication trial should be initiated.

Q: Will the medication change my child's personality?

A: This is a common concern among parents. The goal of treatment with any of the AD/HD medications is treatment of only the AD/HD symptoms. If there is an indication that your child's personality is different, it will be important to evaluate what that means. For example, if your child tended to be impatient, impulsive, and rushed through his school work, those symptoms were probably secondary to his AD/HD symptoms. So, if you start a medication trial and now he is more patient, that is a product of the successful treatment of the AD/HD symptoms, not a change in his personality. Whenever there is a perception that there is a "change in personality," it is essential to determine if that is a true adverse effect, or the successful treatment of the AD/HD symptoms.

Q: My teenager is refusing to take the medication and wants "to be normal." Should I try to force them to take the medication?

A: This is a tough situation, but not an uncommon one. The answer to this question will depend on your teenager's age and the extent of their AD/

HD symptoms. The first thing to remember is to be very patient with your teenager because it is developmentally natural for your teenager to "want to be normal." There will be a great need for helping your teenager understand what AD/HD is, and what it is not. You should gently point out what AD/HD symptoms they exhibit and the negative consequences secondary to those symptoms. You might need to do this repeatedly on your own, as well as with your teenager's doctor. There should be an opportunity for your teenager to ask questions regarding AD/HD as well as regarding the proposed treatment. Their concerns should be taken seriously and addressed accordingly. On many occasions, teenagers have inaccurate information regarding AD/HD or the medications. There is a need to provide accurate and honest information.

The reason for this is that in a few short years, your teenager will be a young adult making their own decisions regarding medical treatment. There might be a short-term value to forcing them to take the medications, but down the road they might become resentful and choose not to take them. Repeatedly pointing out the negative consequences that are a direct result of their AD/HD symptoms will be a far more effective approach long-term.

There are a few situations when safety concerns arise when the teenager doesn't take their medication. This is most obvious regarding the issue of driving. There is a known increased risk of car accidents and violations in teenagers with AD/HD. It is reasonable, therefore, for you to decide that your teenager won't drive unless they are receiving treatment. As a parent, it is your responsibility to make sure that your children and teenagers are safe, so you should explain to them that this is not a punishment, but a safety issue.

Q: Will my daughter become addicted to the medication?

A: The possible addiction to the medication is a common discomfort among many parents. First, you should know that there is a recognized increased risk for alcohol and drug abuse in adolescents with untreated AD/HD. Many studies have consistently shown that medication treatment, including stimulants, actually lowers the risk for alcohol and drug abuse. It is important to differentiate between "needing to take the medication" and "being addicted." For example, a person who has diabetes might need to take insulin on a daily basis. That does not mean they are addicted to it. Addiction implies abuse - not taking the medication the way it is prescribed (in other words, taking too much of the medication in an inappropriate fashion). Another aspect of addiction is when a person has a physical or psychological dependence on the medication; on the contrary, children and teenagers with AD/HD often tend to forget to take their medication. Teenagers can find ways of abusing any type of drug, but the current data appears clear that stimulant medications actually lower the risk of alcohol and drug abuse in teenagers with AD/HD.

Q: My son has always struggled with knowing how to study. We started a medication trial to treat his AD/HD. Will this medication help him improve his study skills?

A: Knowing how to study is a skill that must be learned. The medication is not going to magically help him know how to study. The medication can potentially help the AD/HD symptoms that hamper his ability to study; however, he will need to be taught the skill of studying. It would probably be best if he worked with an organizational coach in a formal way to help develop those skills. The medication can potentially make the acquisition of those skills more successful due to enhanced attention and concentration. This applies to any other set of skills that your teenager needs to learn. The medications are not going to automatically give your teenager capabilities and skills that he doesn't already have. The medications only treat the underlying AD/HD symptoms that interfere with the attainment of some of those learned skills. This, in turn, can lead to progress in a range of areas such as school or job performance.

Q: My son is currently being treated with medication for his AD/HD. Should we give it to him on weekends?

A: If your son is receiving a non-stimulant, he needs to continue taking the medication on a daily basis, regardless of what day of the week it is. The non-stimulants work based on achieving a steady level in the body, so they needed to be taken daily.

The more difficult decision is if your son is receiving a stimulant medication. Stimulants do not need to be taken on a daily basis in order to be effective. However, most children continue to engage in many activities (sports, being with friends, driving, school work, family trips, etc.) during the weekend. AD/HD is a condition that affects all aspects of your son's life, so in most cases, it is recommended that your son take the medication on the weekends.

There are some exceptions to this recommendation. If there are concerns regarding significant weight loss, sometimes it is wise to give either a lower dose of the stimulant, or none at all, on the weekends. There are also some scenarios where children with AD/HD are able to function very well in certain settings without the medication. Each case needs to be evaluated on an individual basis, and of course, should be discussed with your son's physician.

Q: My child has been started on a medication to treat his AD/HD. How do we monitor his progress?

A: You and your child should have regular follow-up visits with your child's prescribing physician. The physician will assess your child at each visit for the presence of any adverse effects secondary to the medication treatment. It is also valuable to utilize certain AD/HD checklists to monitor progress. These checklists can be done before you start the medication, and periodically during treatment. Your child's physician can provide you with copies of the checklists that he/she utilizes to monitor progress. These checklists can be filled out by you, teachers at school, or any other adult who regularly comes into contact with your child, such as a tutor or coach.

SECTION 5—Helpful References and Resources for Further Study

Table 1: Stimulant Medications Table

Chemical Name	Brand Name	Doses	Length of Action
Methylphenidate	Concerta	18mg 27mg 36mg 54mg	Up to 12 hours
	Ritalin LA	10mg 20mg 30mg 40mg	Up to 8 hours
	Metadate CD	10mg 20mg 30mg	Up to 8 hours
	Ritalin	5mg 10mg 20mg	Up to 4 hours
	Methylin	5mg 10mg 20mg	Up to 4 hours
Dexmethylphenidate	Focalin	2.5mg 5mg 10mg	Up to 4 hours
	Focalin XR	5mg 10mg 20mg	Up to 12 hours

Chemical Name	Brand Name	Doses	Length of Action
Dextroamphetamine	Dexedrine	5mg 10mg	Up to 4 hours
	Dexedrine Spansules	5mg 10mg 15mg	Up to 8 hours
Mixed Amphetamine Salts	Adderall XR	5mg 10mg 15mg 20mg 25mg 30mg	Up to 12 hours
	Adderall	5mg 10mg 20mg 30mg	Up to 6 hours

Table 2: Non-Stimulant Medications Table

Chemical Name	Brand Name	Doses
Atomoxetine	Strattera	10 mg 18 mg 25 mg 40 mg 60 mg
Bupropion	Wellbutrin	75 mg 100 mg
	Wellbutrin SR	100 mg 150 mg
	Wellbutrin XL	150 mg 300 mg
Guanfacine	Tenex	1 mg 2 mg
Clonidine	Catapres	0.1 mg 0.2 mg 0.3 mg

References

Alexander-Roberts, C. *ADHD and Teens: A parent's guide to making it through the tough years*. Lanham, Maryland: Taylor Trade Publishing, 1995.

American Academy of Child and Adolescent Psychiatry. "Practice parameter for the use of stimulant medications in the treatment of children, adolescents, and adults." *Journal of the American Academy of Child and Adolescent Psychiatry* 41 (2002): 26S–49S.

American Psychiatric Association. *Diagnostic and statistical manual of mental disorders (DSM-IV-TR) 4th edition text revised*. Washington, DC: American Psychiatric Press, 2000.

Barkley, R. *ADHD and the nature of self-control*. New York: Guilford Press, 1997.

Biederman, J., R. Baldessarini, V. Wright, D. Knee, and J. Harmatz. "A double-blind placebo controlled study of Desipramine in the treatment of ADD: I. Efficacy." *Journal of the American Academy of Child and Adolescent Psychiatry.* 28 (1989): 777–784.

Biederman, J., and A. Horton. *Adderall XR and attention deficit hyperactivity disorder*. Hoboken, New Jersey: Science Press Inc., 2002.

Biederman, J., J. Newcorn, and S. Sprich. "Comorbidity of attention-deficit hyperactivity disorder with conduct, depressive, anxiety, and other disorders." *American Journal of Psychiatry.* 148 (1991): 564–577.

Bradley, C. "The behavior of children receiving Benzedrine." *American Journal of Psychiatry*. 94 (1937): 577–585.

Chacko, A., W. E. Pelham, E. M. Gnagy, A. Greiner, G. Vallano, O. Bukstein, and M. Rancurello. "Stimulant medication effects in a summer treatment program among young children with attention-deficit/hyperactivity disorder." *Journal of the American Academy of Child and Adolescent Psychiatry.* 2005: 249–257.

Conners, C. K., C.D. Casat, C. T. Gualtieri, et al. "Bupropion hydrochloride in attention deficit disorder with hyperactivity." *Journal of the American Academy of Child and Adolescent Psychiatry.* 35 (1996): 1314–1321.

Cox, D.J., R.L. Merkel, J.K. Penberthy, B. Kovatchev, and C.S. Hankin. "Impact of methylphenidate delivery profiles on driving performance of adolescents with attention-deficit/ hyperactivity disorder: a pilot study." *Journal of the American Academy of Child and Adolescent Psychiatry.* 43 (2004): 269–275.

Daly, J., and T. Wilens. "The use of tricyclic antidepressants in children and adolescents." *Pediatric Clinics of North America.* 45 (1998): 1123–1135.

Daviss, W. B., P. Bentivoglio, R. Racusin, K.M. Brown, J.Q. Bostic, and L. Wiley. "Bupropion sustained release in adolescents with comorbid attention-deficit/ hyperactivity disorder and depression." *Journal of the American Academy of Child and Adolescent Psychiatry.* 40 (2001): 307–314.

Department of Health and Human Services. *Attention Deficit Hyperactivity Disorder*. National Institutes of Health, September 2003.

Elia, J. "Attention deficit/hyperactivity disorder: Pharmacotherapy." *Psychiatry.* 2 (2005): 27–35.

"Expert Roundtable Highlights: Stimulants and Atomoxetine in the treatment of attention-deficit/hyperactivity disorder." *The Journal of Clinical Psychiatry.* Monograph 2004, Volume 19.

Faraone, S., and T. Wilens. "Does stimulant treatment lead to substance use disorders?" *Journal of Clinical Psychiatry.* 64.11 (2003): 9–13.

"FDA Issues Suicide Warning on ADHD Drug." *consumeraffairs.com*. 29 Sept. 2005. <*www.consumeraffairs.com/news04/2005/fda_strattera.html*>. 6 Oct. 2005.

"FDA Statement: Statement on Adderall." *U.S. Food and Drug Administation*. 9 Feb. 2005. <*www.fda.gov/ bbs/topics/news/2005/NEW01156.html*>. 9 Feb. 2005.

"FDA Talk Paper: New Warning for Strattera." *U.S. Food and Drug Administation*. 17 Dec. 2004. <*www.fda.gov/bbs/topics/ANSWERS/2004/ANS01335.htm*>. 21 Dec. 2004.

Green, W. *Child and Adolescent Clinical Psychopharmacology, 2nd Edition*. Baltimore, Maryland: Williams & Wilkins, 1995.

Green, W. "The treatment of attention-deficit hyperactivity disorder with non-stimulant medications." *Child and Adolescent Psychiatric Clinics of North America*. 4 (1995): 169–195.

"Health Canada Allows Adderall XR back on the Canadian Market." *Health Canada*. 24 Aug. 2005. <*www.hc-sc.gc.ca/ahc-asc/media/nr-cp/2005/2005_92_ e.html*>. 22 Sept. 2005.

Hechtman, L. "Assessment and diagnosis of attention-deficit/hyperactivity disorder." *Child and Adolescent Psychiatric Clinics of North America*. 9 (2000): 481–498.

Hunt, R., A. Arnste, and M. Asbell. "An open trial of Guanfacine in the treatment of attention-deficit/hyperactivity disorder." *Journal of the American Academy of Child and Adolescent Psychiatry*. 34 (1995): 50–54.

Hunt, R., R. B. Minderaa, and D. J. Cohen. "The therapeutic effect of clonidine in attention deficit disorder with hyperactivity: A comparison with placebo and methylphenidate." *Psychopharmacology Bulletin*. 22 (1986): 229–236.

James, R., and W. Sharp. "Double-blind, placebo-controlled study of single-dose amphetamine formulation in ADHD." *Journal of the American Academy of Child and Adolescent Psychiatry.* 40 (2001): 1268–1276.

Klein, R., B. Landa, J. Mattes, and D. Klein. "Methylphenidate and growth in hyperactive children: A controlled withdrawal study." *Archives of General Psychiatry.* 45 (1988): 1127–1130.

Klein, R., and S. Mannuzza. "Hyperactive boys almost grown up: III. Methylphenidate effects on ultimate height." *Archives of General Psychiatry.* 45 (1988): 1131–1134.

Kluger, J. "Medicating young minds: Drugs have become increasingly popular for treating kids with mood and behavior problems. But how will that affect them in the long run?" *Time.* 2003, November 3rd.

Michelson, D., A. Allen, J. Busner, et al. "Once-daily atomoxetine treatment for children and adolescents with attention-deficit hyperactivity disorder: a randomized, placebo-controlled study." *American Journal of Psychiatry.* 159 (2002):1896–1901.

Motavalli, Mukaddes N., and O. Abali. "Venlafaxine in children and adolescents with attention-deficit hyperactivity disorder." *Psychiatric Clinic Neurosciences.* 58 (2004): 92–95.

MTA Cooperative Group. "Changes in effectiveness and growth during the follow-up phase of the NIMH-MTA study." *Pediatrics.* 113 (2004): 762–769.

MTA Cooperative Study. "14-month randomized clinical trial of treatment strategies for attention deficit hyperactivity disorder." *Archives of General Psychiatry.* 56 (1999): 1073–1086.

MTA Cooperative Study. "Moderators and mediators of treatment response for children with ADHD: the MTA study." *Archives of General Psychiatry.* 56 (1999): 1088–1096.

Novartis Pharmaceuticals Corporation. *Prescribing Information—Focalin XR (dexmethylphenidate hydrochloride) extended-release capsules.* East Hanover, New Jersey. May 2005.

Olvera, R. L., S. R. Pliszka, J. Luh, and R. Tatum. "An open trial of venlafaxine in the treatment of attention-deficit/hyperactivity disorder in children and adolescents." *Journal of Child and Adolescent Psychopharmacology.* 6 (1996): 241–250.

Pliszka, S. R. "Non-stimulant treatment of attention-deficit/hyperactivity disorder." *CNS Spectrums.* 8 (2003): 253–258.

Prince, J. B., T. E. Wilens, J. Biederman, et al. "A controlled study of nortriptyline in children and adolescents with attention deficit hyperactivity disorder." *Journal of Child and Adolescent Psychopharmacology.* 10 (2000): 193–204.

"Public Health Advisory for Adderall and Adderall XR." *U.S. Food and Drug Administation.* 9 Feb. 2005. <*www.fda.gov/cder/drug/advisory/adderall.htm*>. 16 Feb. 2005.

Riddle, M., J. Nelson, C. Kleinman, et al. "Sudden death in children receiving Norpramin: a review of three reported cases and commentary." *Journal of the American Academy of Child and Adolescent Psychiatry.* 30 (1991): 104–108.

Roman, T., C. Szobot, S. Martins, J. Biederman, L. A. Rohde, and M. H. Hutz. "Dopamine transporter gene and response to methylphenidate in attention-deficit/hyperactivity disorder." *Pharmacogenetics.* 12 (2002): 497–499.

Rugino, T. A., and T. C. Samsock. "Modafinil in children with attention-deficit hyperactivity disorder." *Pediatric Neurology.* 29 (2003): 136–142.

Scahill, L., P. Chappell, Y. Kim, et al. "A placebo-controlled study of Guanfacine in the treatment of children with tic disorders and attention deficit hyperactivity disorder." *American Journal of Psychiatry.* 158 (2001): 1067–1074.

Short, E., M. Manos, R. Findling, and E. Schubel. "A prospective study of stimulant response in preschool children: insights from ROC analyses." *Journal of the American Academy of Child and Adolescent Psychiatry*. 43 (2004): 251–259.

Singer, H., J. Brown, S. Quaskey, L. Rosenberg, E. Mellits, and M. Denckla. "The treatment of attention-deficit hyperactivity disorder in Tourette's syndrome: a double-blind placebo-controlled study with Clonidine and Desipramine." *Pediatrics.* 95 (1995): 74–81.

Swanson, J., D. Flockhart, D. Urea, D. Cantwell, D. Connor, and L. Williams. "Clonidine in the treatment of ADHD: questions about safety and efficacy." *Journal of Child and Adolescent Psychopharmacology.* 5 (1995): 301–304.

Taylor, F., and J. Russo. "Efficacy of Modafinil compared to Dextroamphetamine for the treatment of attention deficit hyperactivity disorder in adults." *Journal of Child and Adolescent Psychopharmacology.* 10 (2000): 311–320.

Tourette's Syndrome Study Group. "Treatment of ADHD in children with tics: a randomized controlled trial." *Neurology.* 58 (2002): 527–536.

Turner, D., L. Clark, J. Dowson, T. W, Robbins, and B. Sahakian. "Modafinil improves cognition and response inhibition in adult attention-deficit/ hyperactivity disorder." *Biological Psychiatry.* 55 (2004): 1031–1040.

Vitiello, B. "Psychopharmacology for young children: Clinical needs and research opportunities." *Pediatrics.* 108 (2001): 983–989.

Wachter, K. "ADHD drug eases anxiety, not depression." *Clinical Psychiatry News.* August 2005; 44

Wilens, T. E. "Attention-deficit/hyperactivity disorder and the substance use disorders: the nature of the relationship, subtypes at risk, and treatment issues." *Psychiatric Clinics of North America.* 27 (2004): 283–301.

Wilens, T. *Straight Talk about Psychiatric Medications For Kids.* New York: The Guilford Press, 2004.

Wilens, T., and W. Pelham. "ADHD treatment with once-daily OROS methylphenidate: Interim 12-month results from a long-term open label study." *Journal of the American Academy of Child and Adolescent Psychiatry.* 42 (2003): 424–433.

Zito, J., D. Safer, S. dosReis, J. Gardner, M. Boles, and F. Lynch. "Trends in the prescribing of psychotropic medication to preschoolers." *Journal of the American Medical Association.* 283 (2000): 1025–1030.

Books to consider for further study:

American Psychiatric Association. *Diagnostic and Statistical Manual of Mental Disorders (DSM-IV-TR) 4th edition text revised.* Washington, DC: American Psychiatric Association, 2000.

Barkley, Russell A. *Taking Charge of ADHD.* New York: The Guilford Press, 2000.

Greene, R. W. *The Explosive Child: A New Approach for Understanding and Parenting Easily Frustrated, "Chronically Inflexible" Children.* New York: Harper Collins, 1998.

Hallowell, E. M., and J. J. Ratey. *Driven to Distraction.* New York: Pantheon Books, 1994.

Wilens, Timothy E. *Straight Talk About Psychiatric Medications For Kids.* New York: The Guilford Press, 2004.

Web Sites

http://www.addwarehouse.com

- A great resource for numerous materials for AD/HD and other related issues

http://www.chadd.org

- Comprehensive web site of the largest AD/HD organization: Children and Adults with Attention-Deficit/Hyperactivity Disorder (CHADD)

http://www.additudemag.com

- Site sponsored by ADDitude Magazine - a national monthly magazine
- Many valuable articles covering a wide range of issues related to AD/HD

http://www.nimh.nih.gov

- Site for National Institute of Mental Health
- Valuable resource for current research results and studies

http://www.add.org

- Site for Attention Deficit Disorder Association (ADDA)—focusing on Adult AD/HD

http://www.addresources.org

- Comprehensive list of links
- Resource for finding providers
- Online book store
- AD/HD Skill-Building Tele-courses

http://www.aacap.org

- Site for The American Academy of Child and Adolescent Psychiatry
- Excellent source for educational materials
- Provides *Facts For Families* as a resource on a variety of topics including AD/HD and medication treatment
- Resource for locating a Child and Adolescent Psychiatrist in your area

http://www.aap.org

- Site for The American Academy of Pediatrics
- Many educational materials

http://www.psych.org

- Website for the American Psychiatric Association
- Provides numerous resources and information

http://www.ncld.org

- Website of The National Center for Learning Disabilities
- Resource for information on Learning Disabilities
- Information on advocacy
- Comprehensive list of links to other valuable resources and organizations

http://www.americoach.org

- Website of The American Coaching Association
- Provides a list of coaches in your local area

http://www.ldanatl.org

- Website of The Learning Disabilities Association of America (LDA)
- Provides information for parents, teachers, and professionals
- Has valuable resources, as well as a bookstore

Organizations

Children and Adults with Attention–Deficit / Hyperactivity Disorder (CHADD)

- Largest organization serving individuals with AD/HD
- Holds annual conference
- Publishes "Attention" magazine
- Has professional directory
- Local Chapters
- National Resource Center on AD/HD
- Contact Information:
  8181 Professional Place
  Suite 150
  Landover, MD 20785
  Phone: 800-233-4050
  Fax: 301-306-7090
  Website: www.chadd.org

American Academy of Child & Adolescent Psychiatry (AACAP)

- Leading professional medical association of Child and Adolescent Psychiatrists
- A resource of current research on psychiatric illnesses affecting children and adolescents
- Provides practice guidelines for providers
- FACT sheets for families
- Contact Information:
  3615 Wisconsin Avenue NW
  Washington, DC 20016-3007
  Phone: 202-966-7300
  Fax: 202-966-2891
  Website: www.aacap.org

Learning Disabilities Association of America (LDA)

- Provides support for parents, teachers, and professionals
- Has local chapters in every state
- Contact Information:
  4156 Library Road
  Pittsburgh, PA 15234
  Phone: 412-341-1515
  Fax: 412-344-0224
  Website: www.ldanatl.org

National Center for Learning Disabilities (NCLD)

- Excellent source of information and resources
- Provides referral sources
- Effective advocate for fair policies
- Contact Information:
  381 Park Avenue South
  Suite 1401
  New York, NY 10016
  Phone: 212-545-7510
  Fax: 212-545-9665
  Website: www.ncld.org

American Coaching Association

- AD/HD coaches can help students with a variety of essential skills such as time and space management, setting priorities, organizational skills, and study skills.
- Contact Information:
  P. O. Box 353
  Lafayette Hill, PA 19144
  Phone: 610-825-8572
  Fax: 610-825-4505
  Website: www.americoach.org

American Academy of Pediatrics

- National organization of pediatricians
- A good source of educational materials
- Contact Information:
  141 Northwest Point Boulevard
  Elk Grove Village, IL 60007-1098
  Phone 847-434-4000
  Website: www.aap.org

Compiled List of Rules

RULE # 1 Before talking to your child or teenager's physician about starting medications, you need to know what the diagnosis is, and how the diagnosis was determined.

RULE # 2 Medications are not the only treatment option for AD/HD, and they work best when combined with other forms of treatment.

RULE # 3 Medication treatment should be considered only if the AD/HD symptoms are currently impairing the child's function.

RULE # 4 The potential benefits of the medication need to outweigh the potential risks of adverse effects.

RULE # 5 Keep detailed records of all medications that your child has taken.

RULE # 6 Give an accurate and detailed family history.

RULE # 7 Some medications have the potential to worsen underlying problems.

RULE # 8 Not everything that happens while your child is on medicine is because of the medicine.

RULE # 9 Don't expect medications to fix every symptom.

RULE # 10 Having a side effect does not always mean it is necessary to stop the medication.

RULE # 11 The medication dosage amount is important.

RULE # 12 Medications that are not specifically FDA-approved for children can still be used by children in certain situations.

RULE # 13 Tell your physician all of the medications that your child is on, including over-the-counter medications and "natural" or "herbal" medications.

RULE # 14 Involve your adolescent in the discussions about medications, and be patient with them through the process.

RULE # 15 For most children, parents should be responsible for administering the medications; starting in the mid- to late-teens, most teenagers can begin to assume some of that responsibility.

RULE # 16 Don't look for a quick fix; be patient.

RULE # 17 Begin new medications only when at least one parent is available to monitor any negative effects.

RULE # 18 Closely note baseline sleep, appetite, and mood prior to initiating a medication trial.

RULE # 19 The more times a medicine needs to be taken, the higher the risk of missing a dose.

RULE # 20 Lack of effectiveness of a medication does not mean that the diagnosis is incorrect.

RULE # 21 Don't feel under pressure to make an urgent decision regarding the use of medications for your child.

Index

Author Biography

Dr. Mohab Hanna is a board-certified Child and Adolescent Psychiatrist in private practice in Lutherville, Maryland. He completed his training in Child & Adolescent Psychiatry at the Johns Hopkins University School of Medicine in Baltimore, Maryland. Dr. Hanna completed his training in general psychiatry at the University of Medicine & Dentistry of New Jersey (UMDNJ)–New Jersey Medical School. Dr. Hanna worked as a Child and Adolescent Psychiatrist at The Kennedy Krieger Institute—an affiliate of the Johns Hopkins University School of Medicine—for two years, specializing in the treatment of children and adolescents with developmental disabilities. In addition, Dr. Hanna was on the faculty of the Johns Hopkins University School of Medicine for two years at the Clinical Instructor level. He is a member of AACAP (The American Academy of Child & Adolescent Psychiatry) and CHADD (Children & Adults With Attention-Deficit/Hyperactivity Disorder).